A Cat Called Canoe

Ron Stob

with Eva I. Stob

Raven Cove Publishing
Greenback, Tennessee

Dedication

To the cats from our past that became our extended family, and to our children who possessed and were possessed by cats.

Midnight was Eva's companion when she was a girl growing up in Arkansas. It was so long ago she doesn't remember what color he was. Oh, yeah, it was black.

Luther and Katie, named after the German Reformer, Martin Luther and his wife Kathryn, were the companions of the Stob kids on Liberty Street in Chicago. This began a lifetime of cat caring for five kids.

Ebony and Buffy, litter-mates, came to live with Eva and kids in Tucson, then moved with them to Arroyo Grande, California, along with two poodles, two horses and a bird. Buffy lived to the ripe old age of 17 in spite of being hung on the garage door and hit by a car. Ron convinced Eva he really did like this cat despite his accidental involvement with both incidents.

Daisy and *Beauregard* and a half dozen other kittens followed young Alan home after school one day. These two were chosen; the others charmed their way into new homes by being cute in front of the local supermarket. Daisy disappeared before long, but Beau stayed around until a move into town upset his routine.

Hamilton, named after Grandpa Stob's dairy, was daughter Laura's first cat outside the parental home in Chicago. Laura later moved with *Katie* to Colorado where she showed a preference for a family in the neighborhood "who never liked cats." The couple "who didn't like cats" even buried Katie in a grave marked with a tombstone.

Cleopatra, with green eyes and a red nose, was aristocratic and lady-like and belonged to Laura who was by now back in Chicago. *Mac Attack*, a refugee from the dormitory of strays at the shelter, was supposed to be a guy's cat, but *Mac* turned out to be a crybaby and Laura ended up sleeping with *Mac* instead of husband Tim. Then daughter Zoe "kidnapped" *Mac* and turned him upside down and sidewise and tossed him around and *Mac* said, "I like her best."

Tubeleaux is a cat who came in out of the cold after trying to eke out a living at Trout Lake, Colorado, 10,000 feet above sea level during the winter when the temperature was "two below" zero. After being put out of Greg and Tracy's cabin, she wandered awhile and returned a second time with a pitiful need. Further emaciated and destitute Greg and Tracy couldn't turn their backs and took her in again – this time for good. Not until the mountain was green with spring did she dare leave the cabin.

Gandolf was big. I had given son Phil a charming little Himalayan with blue eyes whom we called *Frank*. But Phil wanted a big cat so he gave *Frank* away as a wedding gift and adopted *Gandolf*. Gandolf loved to be whacked, like swatting a rug. Honest. Wherever Phil lived on the coast of California, Gandolf was by his side. It was heartbreaking to see Phil's grief when *Gandolf* died.

Phil married Janis who "talks with animals," especially cats. *Zoe* and *Lulu* were garden fixtures for many years in their Fremont, California, home. Now Zoe is pushing up petunias, Lulu teeters with age and *Tigger* is the newcomer, an aloof member of the family.

Gromit and *Kelty* inherited Jeff and Dawn in Vancouver, Washington. They check out the territory from roof tops and have been known to lie in the gutter. 'Happens in Vancouver.

Ruphus and *De Chelly*, one congenial and comfortable, the other reticent and shy, live with daughter Amy and Brad and baby Erin in Albuquerque. All of New Mexico is a sandbox. These two cats have it made.

Acknowledgments

A writer is a voice calling in the wilderness without his critics, tutors and teachers. We went back to the well and solicited the comments of readers and writers and editors who have helped us in the past. Without their input our stories would be untested recipes, dishes that have never been sampled.

We thank Don McGuire, organist, reader and a guy with a penchant for the small stuff we would have missed. Our gratitude to Katie Bryant, cat keeper, reader and writer who cleaned us up a bit and made us respectable. Kudus to Jessie Peterson Jones, English teacher, writer, who knew how to use a red pen. Boy, she's tough. To sister Joyce Kane, lover of animals and words, and our gentle counselor.

Endless praise for my wife Eva who laughed with me, offered herself and Canoe as subjects, took great pleasure in reading and rewriting our episodes and then took the raw material and created a book.

Eva is what I'm not – computer literate, attentive to detail and long suffering. I'm a wild carp on a thin line and it's her job to land the monster, remove the barbs from his mouth and bring him to the table in a savory aspect. The labor and suffering involved in getting this book to the shelf saved me from anonymity and gave me a voice that otherwise would never be heard.

Contents

Prologue

Picking a Human: The Cat's Point of View

It's usually the human looking at the animal, scrutinizing the coat, searching for a look in the eyes, analyzing the approach. Maybe it's the calm of the animal or its sinuous sidling. Maybe it's the fetching look, the texture of the coat, the color of the eyes, the similarity this animal has with previous animals of one's experience. We search for chemistry, something in the animal's behavior that says, "That's the one."

But what's the animal point of view? What are they looking for in an adoptive friend and fellow traveler?

Unattached cats like to be romanced, talked to, ogled without handling, touched but not grabbed. They want a spiritual relationship before a carnal one. They're like women.

A woman's voice is ringing bells; a guy's voice is timpani. A woman's face is chiffon; a guy's face is sandpaper. Adipose is comfort; muscle is armament.

But some cats have strayed far away from considering life with a human, male or female. They've experienced alley-kicking kids and rough men with little regard for the least of these. They cannot imagine life by the hearth.

Chapter 1

A Strange Name for a Cat

When we were building our cottage on the lake in Tennessee, we lived in our fifth-wheel trailer at the Crosseyed Cricket Campground. We thought a canoe would be fun for exploring the rivers and creeks, so we bought a used canoe for $200. But it turned out to be very tender (tippy). With Eva in the bow and me in the stern, we quivered out onto the lake on our maiden voyage and soon realized that it was a lot like log rolling.

Then a speeding boat came by and sent its wake rushing toward us. The rolling tsunami was about to swamp us, so I turned the canoe and raced for shore. Through deft handling that verged on panic and Olympic-caliber speed paddling, I got the boat to the launch ramp and beached it. Quick as a cat, Eva scampered ashore leaving me in the canoe with the bow pointing heavenward. The first wave hit... then the second and the third.

Sitting on the ramp, swamped and totally soaked, made me feel safer because there was no impending threat, but it was fall and the water was cold. We pulled the canoe on shore, tipped out the water, put it back on the truck and laid the contents of my wallet on the dashboard to dry. The next day we ran an ad in the Thrifty Nickel: "Nifty 12-foot canoe, perfect for adventurous, fun-loving couple with great balance." A couple looking for wet adventures bought it, threw it on their vehicle and we went to the bank with our $200 figuring we'd let the money ripen until we found the right watercraft.

Meanwhile at the campground, a long-haired tuxedo kitten with the baby face of Shirley Temple and the disposition of St. Francis perched on a nearby picnic table. He was sunning himself, looking adorable and putting his coat in order. It was what made him so attractive, a tuxedo in impeccable condition.

He had the patchwork coat of a Holstein, feet like dollops of whipped cream, and a long black bushy tail that he carried like a dust wand. The kitten with big topaz eyes sauntered over to our trailer and looked up at me soulfully and seemed to say, "I like you."

"Whadda ya mean, you like me?" I said. "You don't even know me."

"True, but on cold nights all I have is the flue pipe on the roof of a single-wide trailer to keep me warm (sniff), and when the big horned owl hoots, I know he's looking for me (sob, sniff...sniff...sniff). Maybe if I stayed with you, I wouldn't be so scared."

"Scram before my wife sees you, pussy cat."

Too late.

Eva emerged from the trailer and the kitty approached her with baby-talk-squeaks, gently moving forward while maintaining eye contact. His message to her: "I like you even better than him."

She extended a hand. "Hi, kitty. Aren't you pretty? And

look at that sweet face. Can I hold you?"

Kitty sampled the hands, the high voice, and the tender strokes. "Sure, you can touch me; you can cuddle me; you can smother me with affection."

"Oh, you're a sweetie, but we don't want to be tied down with a pet. Maybe we can just be friends."

Having a cat at this time in our life was never considered. Arguments were stacked against being possessed by an animal (as opposed to "possessing" an animal); but there she was with a cat in her arms and angels were singing.

We took him inside and gave him milk. He appeared healthy and well fed although he was infested with fleas. He explored the trailer and found a place to curl up and take a nap – on my clean folded clothes stacked on a ledge at the head of the bed. When he woke up, he jumped in the bathtub and sent a yellow trickle to the drain. Aha! He had inadvertently answered a question about keeping a cat in a trailer.

He ate more before we put him out. We didn't want to get too attached.

We learned that this kitten was company to many of the people at the campground. He walked up to their motorhomes, accepted food, drank a little wine, smoked cigars with the guys, then watched the rigs drive off and he'd be alone again. Campground cats see a turnstile of human visitors and their affections are shallow. But some of us were permanent. Seasons changed and we were still there.

We were there when he wanted a warm bed or food. He liked us when he was hungry, when it was raining, when autumn leaves fell and sharp winds foretold the advent of winter. He even liked us when the sun shone and there was no immediate need to be sheltered or rescued. We were shoving carrots through the bars and Kitty was on the other side sucking them up. Were we choosing Kitty, or was Kitty choosing us?

We had traced Kitty's comings and goings and knew that he belonged to a young couple that lived through the woods in a single-wide trailer. They had two small kids plus a gray short-haired kitty and "our" kitten with the black and white coat. We'd seen the cats running through the woods together and observed the black and white kitty being picked up by the little boy. This explained his comfort level around people.

On one occasion when we returned the cat to them, the woman in the single-wide trailer said that the cats weren't invited into the house because the litter box became a playground for the kids. So the cats were kept outdoors, snuggling together beneath the trailer and sleeping around the furnace vent pipe on cold nights.

We wouldn't see him for days, then he'd come back and plead with us again. One night he came with a message: "I'm sick."

So we took him in…again, cleaned him up…again, and de-flead him. We put out food but he wouldn't eat. His nose was warm and he was listless. He'd lost weight and looked gaunt. His internal body temperature was dropping and there was urgency for his care.

"What are you doing, Kitty?" we said. "This is no place to die."

We considered our options? Watch him spiral downward? Throw him out and let him take care of himself the best he could? Let him walk out into the woods and lie down in the cold rain?

An inner voice said, "Inasmuch as you've done it to the

least of these, you have done it unto me." Now I know Jesus was exhorting His followers to clothe the naked, visit those in prison and feed the hungry, but somehow the call for compassion seemed to extend to all of God's creatures. We couldn't turn our backs on the kitty.

That night we kept him in our trailer and in the morning he was still alive. We took Kitty back to the single-wide trailer in the woods and asked the young parents if the cat ever had shots.

"No, we don't have money for that," they said. "The cats are on their own. If they get sick, that's their problem. If they die, well… they're only cats." The man's idea of humane treatment for a sick cat was a hammer blow to the head. We cringed.

"He needs to see a vet," we said. "He's sick and we're afraid he's going to die."

"If you want to take him to the vet, that's fine. You can keep him if you want. We just don't have money to spend on cats. You can even have the litter box if you want it."

So we took him to the vet and with calculators running considered the investment in a stranger who was working his way into our affections. We bought the diagnostic service and the leukemia test. I was secretly hoping for a positive reading; then the course of action would be easy. Put him to sleep.

But he tested negative. He had a chance. He was only about seven months old, was beautiful in coat, compliant in nature and forlorn in disposition. We took him home with directions from Dr. Tom Bradbury, the kindly vet who reduced our bill because we were poor in coat, weary in disposition, and kindly toward one of God's creatures. Antibiotics, deworming medication, flea eradication and treatments for every conceivable disease and contagion known to man and beast were prescribed — vaccination for rabies, distemper, leukemia, tuberculosis, diphtheria, bubonic plague, bad breath, malaria, amebic dysentery, polio, meningitis, pneumonia, muscular dystrophy, multiple sclerosis, strep throat, hepatitis, depression, AND a prescribed diet of high cost meats, scrambled eggs, balanced cat chow and lots of cuddling.

All of this cost us somewhere near the value of the canoe that we had just sold. Reflecting on the unplanned change in the direction of our canoe money, Eva, in a cryptic moment said, "Maybe we ought to call him Canoe."

Naming a cat is tantamount to adoption. Unwittingly we had become parents.

Ron and Eva pose with their new cat, Canoe, in front of their 5th-wheel trailer at the Crosseyed Cricket Campground.

Chapter 2

Or Did We Own Him?

As our kitty got better, we became more attached. A cat, or any creature, shouldn't be desirable merely because of the way it looks and moves. What kind of love is that? It's like saying to your spouse, "I'll love you so long as you look like Demi Moore, have the manners of Amy Vanderbilt and the athleticism of Serena Williams."

But a cat gets away with this.

There is a grace in cats that's remarkable. They don't think of soiling your bed. They approach their food like a gourmet going to a bistro and their movements are sinuous and seductive. They murmur for food and cuddle for attention. They know the magic of touch, sliding softly between legs, raising their heads for a solicitous hand and fitting their body into yours. They know seduction without instruction.

Walk softly and act dignified is the message of a cat. They haven't been to Dartmouth, don't appear on the social pages, haven't gone through the school of social graces, don't own a summer home at Newport, have no idea what side of the plate a fork goes, own only one set of clothes and yet they approach any task with dignity, grace and decorum. They make humans look like dolts.

He even smelled good. It was an unusual odor, attractive and alive, his own charisma. It was probably what he imparted to his coat as he doted on himself. He was a contortionist, getting his wet, barbed tongue on every part of his body, except for the top of his head. For that, he'd lick his paws, then wipe them over his head time and again. Cat's spit is obviously good grooming lacquer because he was an outdoor cat that looked impeccable.

During those fall and winter days when we were building the house on Tellico Lake and living in our fifth-wheel trailer, I walked each morning down the gravel road through the woods to get the newspaper. One morning I took Canoe along, trying to train him to accompany me on walks. To some extent it worked, but I quickly re-learned the way of cats...follow for a while...stop and watch falling leaves...saunter, saunter, saunter...stop...lick a paw...chase a bug...look back...become a statue.

I called and slapped my thighs, "C'mon, Canoe, C'mon." He looked as if I was loony, turned his head away, then bound past me like lightning, a streak of feline exuberance. Then he cooled down as if he was quick-frozen. I caught up, scratched his head, picked him up, cuddled him and put him down again. I was twenty yards down the road and he was still sitting there. I called, he looked, I called and slapped my thighs, he looked. Then without rhyme or reason his start button got punched and he came. "I'll come at my rate...if I care to come at all," was the message.

I was trying to get in an aerobic walk. The cat would only saunter, which was cute, his little white paws touching the gravel in the most endearing way, but I was being taken in with this cute crap. What's wrong with me? I'm mature; I've been around.

I walked faster, putting distance between Canoe and myself who continued to move at lukewarm speeds…saunter, saunter, saunter.

"Time to lick my bottom."

"Now I'm never going to cuddle you," I called back to him.

"Look at that bird," he says.

"C'mon, Canoe, I don't have all day."

I went back and picked him up. An old work truck at the campground came by and Canoe stiffened as the truck approached, then clawed his way out of my grasp and headed for the woods. The truck passed and I stood with empty arms looking like a person expecting a sky drop. The truck slowed, the driver looked quizzically, then moved on. Canoe meanwhile, was crouched somewhere in the woods. I went looking, peeling away the complex and thorny understory.

He came to me obligingly and we walked together until we were down by the pond where the big gray goose and the ducks were squawking. This was new to Canoe. His usual rounds were up the hill by our trailer and the nearby trailer with the snot-nosed kids, but he made no attempt to leave me. When the ducks swam to our side of the pond, I put him down so he could see and smell these other creatures of the world. The ducks approached us boldly as if we had food for them. The summer campers were gone and this could be their last handout until spring. Canoe quickly cowered behind me like a child on the first day of kindergarten. This four-pound male cat was not ready for birds as big as he was. I picked him up and we proceeded to the mailbox and back up the gravel road toward our fifth wheel trailer in the woods.

I put Canoe down for the last 50 yards of our walk. It was the same style of lagging behind, being distracted by a world that should not have looked this new. This was an alley cat that was supposed to be used to the ways of the wild, and this was his territory, but every tree was something to sink his claws into, each fluttering leaf a novel toy, each squawking game bird an animated toy. In one of his streaks of excitement he climbed a dogwood tree with such speed I thought he had overcome gravity. He was 8 feet off the ground and onto a limb the size of one of his legs. He teetered and swayed and looked back and said, "Ohhhhhh, how do I get out of this?"

"It's your problem, Canoe. I'm not going to shinny up a tree to get you down."

I walked on, trying to be indifferent, but I behaved like an anxious parent. I glanced back and saw a black and white body swaying from a limb like a pendulum, then I saw him inch back to the trunk and drop to the ground.

"C'mon, Canoe," I called.

A black and white comet shot by me. We were together again.

Then I lost him under a clump of prostrate junipers where chickadees were scolding him. I could not coax him out, nor could I go in and get him. But in another instant he shot out and ran toward the trailer where I caught up to him and brought him inside.

Now he's sitting on the top of the printer as I write and he's found the Venetian blind wand worth swatting. He also discovered that the nearby drapes with their string-like construction catch his claws, so I leave you with the image of a black and white cat hanging by one paw and trying to figure out how to disengage. I'm not going to lift a finger.

"Oh, wait, Kitty. I'll help you."

It's so hard to be tough.

Chapter 3

He's Ungrateful, Inconsiderate and Short Sighted

Sunday was a beautiful day. Temperatures were in the sixties and Canoe jumped out the door when we opened it. He ran up trees, stared at squirrels scrounging in the duff for the season's last acorns and walnuts, and chased dropping leaves. Life was good; the cat was happy. Eva and I moved in and out of the trailer doing various things, and when it came time to come inside again, Canoe was gone. We thought we knew where he was – back with his alley cat friend under the single-wide coach inhabited by Kevin, Lynn and their two kids. Sure enough, he had taken up with his feral friend again and they were running through the woods. It would be hard to entice him back home with this kind of playmate nearby, but the little gray cat may be carrying leukemia and rabies and distemper, so he shouldn't be running around with riffraff. We caught him, picked him up and took him home.

But the next time the door opened, Canoe was gone again. We walked to the single-wide coach of Kevin and Lynn and found him, again. We apologized for our intrusion, again, took him home, again, gave him a talkin' to and thought that he was home for the evening. I had to go back out to attach a water line heater and Canoe was nearby. I promised to keep a watch on him, but I got busy and when I looked around for him, he was gone.

I went back to the single-wide trailer where Canoe used to live, but this time he was nowhere around. Dejected, I went home and shut the door on a cat that should know a good deal when he has one. He had free medical, a lunch program, educational and cultural opportunities few cats would ever have, rides in the country and lots of free time to chase balls and catch falling leaves.

The night deepened. Throughout the evening hours Eva or I opened the door, imagining that we'd hear his sweet little "meow." It got cold. Was Canoe under the single-wide with his little friend, getting fleas, grooming her and exchanging cat diseases?

Eva was having a snit about Canoe not coming home. "Doesn't he understand?" she said. "He's got it made here. Look what we've done for him. I'm really disappointed in him."

We talked about his ungratefulness, his inconsideration, his shortsightedness, his stupidity even. He was missing a really good chance to join the middle class, to listen to Mozart and Haydn, to smell cooking aromas of bratwurst and cabbage, to lie indulgently on our bed while we cuddled him and told him how wonderful he was.

In a moment of resignation, Eva recited the lyrics of a poem... "If you love someone, set it free. If it comes back to you, it's yours. If it doesn't, it never was."

Around bedtime, I thought I heard Canoe meow at the door. Of course, this was the fourth time I thought I heard him. I opened the door and Canoe bounded in, his coat standing out to insulate himself from the cold. He went right to his food bowls. No apologies, no excuses, no great affectionate greetings. Just a matter of fact statement, "This is my home. I know it. And no, I don't intend to give you an explanation of where I've been."

That night he had frequent runs to his litter box. His wild diet of bugs, rodents and who knows what else gave him indigestion. I had seen him earlier foraging around a garbage can where he found a slice of quiche with cheese and ham. Maybe this combination of garbage barrel goodies mixed with bugs, mice and moles was playing havoc with his GI. I picked him and smelled him. No mouse smells. No smells at all. This animal never stinks. How does he do it?

In the morning he dirtied himself in the process of not managing diarrhea. Eva and I took him to the sink and washed his bottom like he was a baby. He succumbed to our parental care, lying exposed with his legs apart while we bathed him. We had taken control again.

Now he's running around as if nothing happened. He seems happy to be here and we've become accustomed to his ddjtj883djiwiejjjjf934ujf99u4-09gj… GET OFF THE KEYBOARD, CANOE! …antics and his smiling disposition.

Chapter 4

When Humans Sleep, Cats Play

There is a divider in the fifth wheel that separates the bedroom from the bathroom. This accordion door proved to be cat proof...for two nights. Then Canoe discovered how to get through it. Our nights in bed would have to be shared by a cat. The trick we thought was to get him tired enough so that he'd sleep when we slept. But cats nap, and in a few hours he was ready to play. He'd sit on my chest with his nose on my face, watching my nose hairs move in and out. He'd smell my breath and feel my chest rise and fall. He was the feline rendition of The Thinker. He put his paw on my nose and licked my chin. I awoke and moved him to the floor.

By morning, Canoe had been up a dozen times and back to bed the same number. He played with his tennis ball, walked all the counters, nibbled on the morning's sweet rolls and took a dozen naps. How would we make our schedules jibe?

In the middle of the following night I heard Eva with the cat. Actually, it was only midnight, but I had been asleep for a while. She was on the floor playing with the cat.

"I'm trying to tire him out," she said. "He's bouncing off

the walls, flying around the room, ricocheting across the dinette seats and bounding off the cabinets. He manipulates his tennis ball like Michael Jordan grasps a basketball."

Eva got the grooming brushes out, which further stimulated Canoe. He was laughing and thrumming his hind legs while Eva stroked his fur. He was looking beautiful and his white belly fur was light and fluffy. His eyes danced and you knew there was another uninhibited outburst around the next corner.

Canoe became our early morning wake-up call. He was a soft body treading the bedding. If we as much as opened an eye, it was an invitation. Blinking eyes said, "I love you." He'd lick any hand that was outside the covers, or respond to any movement beneath the sheets. He wanted to get intimate. We wanted to sleep.

It must be a guy thing.

Canoe gives Eva a wake-up call... er, paw.

Chapter 5

Cats Have Timers

We needed to go shopping so we went into the woods and found Canoe and told him we had to go shopping and that he was supposed to go home where we would lock him in the trailer where he'd have nothing to do. Of course, we didn't tell him this, we merely said, "Come here, Canoe. C'mon. Kitty-kitty, c'mon. Please, kitty, kitty, come here. C'mon, Kitty-kitty-kitty. C'mere, meat head, or I'll beat you bloody." He looked, giggled, and ran up a tree. No respect.

Canoe has a set time for play and a time for sleep. When he goes outside to play and run, no matter how we entice him, he will not come to us, obey us or heed our call. He's in his play mode and all receptors to human desires, voices, wishes, demands, exhortations or threats are switched off. He'll look at us with the devil in his eye and run away.

He climbed the tree like a squirrel, getting farther out on a limb until the limb bent with his weight. "Be careful, Canoe," Eva shouted. "You're going to fall." Canoe didn't flinch. I turned my back on him saying in effect, "You're on your own, pussy cat. If you can't crawl down, jump down." He jumped.

We tried again to call him in. Obviously his timer hadn't run out yet, but five minutes later it did and he came as if he knew all the while that he was wanted. Cats have their own clock and they neither know nor care what's on your schedule.

Here's how a cat spends his day: 80% sleeping, 3% terrorist activities, 2% chasing moths, skinks, snowflakes and butterflies, 4.5% watching birds, squirrels, falling leaves and anything else that moves, 5% eating, thinking of food, hunting for food, begging for food, rummaging through garbage for food, 5% coming and going and 0.5% attending to his human companions who pay the rent, provide the food, the medical and the love.

For 0.5% we're willing to put up with this cat. That's a lot of investment for a meager amount of reciprocal affection.

How Cats Spend Their Days

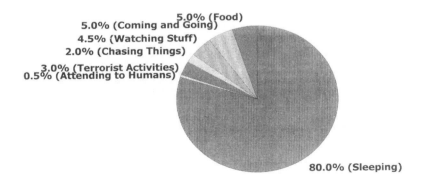

Chapter 6

It's No Great Feet

I saw him go over the edge, clinging with his front claws while his body slowly slid to the floor. We were playing "Attack The Toes," a game of rough tumbling wherein he eats my toes through the bed comforter and I keep changing position. I wiggle my toes and he pounces. I change the position of my feet and he anticipates new wiggles in new places. I sweep my feet from one side of the bed to the other and Canoe rides the waves as my feet pass under him. I increase the speed until he's having a thrill ride. Eventually I win and he's tossed off the bed.

He bounds back on the bed for more adventures in biting stinky toes. He gets so excited, he leaps across the bed, ricochets off the wall, comes back across the bed like a comet, lays like he's dead (with the devil in his eyes and his pupils dilated), then bounds like a coiled spring for my toes, or to the top of the bed to bite Eva's nose. His little brain is in the fun/attack mode. Then just as quickly he'll become a lover and want to be coddled.

Cats are nuts.

Chapter 7

Now You See Him. Now You Don't

Exploring is to a cat what sex is to a teenager – an insatiable curiosity. When I saw Canoe on the back of the trailer's couch slipping purposefully between the wall and the couch, I knew he was seeking new frontiers.

There was no way for him to get out from this hiding place short of pulling open the bottom of the sofa bed. But when I did that, he was nowhere to be seen.

The storage compartments in the trailer had become Canoe's underground. Eva fretted about this while I read the paper, and after a while her maternal angst got the better of her and she impatiently wondered aloud why I was not fretting also. "Look, dear, if you're concerned, go outside, open the basement doors and I'll bet you'll find him in the cabinets that lie beneath our bed."

"But I don't have any shoes on."

"Well, neither do I, but mine are outside and you can slip into them if you're really concerned."

How's that for taking care of my sweetie? I know, pretty indifferent, but I thought that Canoe would satisfy his curiosity after a while and reappear as mysteriously as he disappeared.

Eva went outside and opened the compartment doors and there he was in the back behind the vacuum cleaner and boxes of camper gear.

"C'mere, Canoe. C'mon, get out of there. Come to me. Come on, Canoe. CANOE, COME HERE!" she called.

He looked at her with a cat's way of spitting in your face.

"In my own good time, I'll come out. Maybe I'll live down here for years, who knows?"

Eva came back in and waited for pleading meows. It didn't happen. He probably went to sleep; but in his own  time he came and pressed his face to the grate of the furnace cold air return and looked. He would have made more points if he'd pleaded, meowed, looked distressed and called out, "Mommy, Mommy." Eva asked me to drop the front apron of the couch which allowed her to grab him and take him into her arms. The catch was successful but there was no gratitude on the part of Canoe. She hugged him and he looked away as if he was a teenage boy at school being hugged by his Mom.

When you hug cats, they look away; but if you're lying in bed and the cat comes to YOU, you can expect kneading, purring and a kiss just when you're not asking for one. What kind of a relationship is this?

Chapter 8

Canoe Surfs The Web

The faint light of the computer screen saver is our night light in the trailer. When you move the mouse or touch the keyboard the screen lights up to the opening Microsoft screen. Often at night Canoe goes foraging, walking on the keyboard or touching the mouse. He likes that because our screen saver has words that flow across the screen from right to left. "Somebody wuvs you; I wonder who," it says in a continuous scrolling marquee.

Canoe was fascinated with this moving display and he'd stand on the chair or on the desk and watch the words come onto the screen from the right and disappear off the left side. He couldn't figure it out. He'd watch the words run off, then look behind the monitor to see where they went.

He's perplexed with another phenomenon. The Hewlett Packard printer feeds paper from a lower tray to the printing drum and then to an upper tray. Canoe can't figure out where that paper comes from. He stands like a sentry at the printer watching the paper come out but can't imagine its origin. He puts his paws deep into the printer to see if he can feel where the paper is coming from, or he'll jump on top of the printer and look at the back. Then as if a light went out, he'll hop down and go to his food dish or milk bowl. Milk is good when you're frustrated.

Chapter 9

It's Time To Play Hockey!

Canoe spent most of a sunny Sunday in the trailer with us while Eva paid bills and undertook her bi-weekly nail preparation. Evening came, and we went to bed, but Canoe was just awaking from his long afternoon nap.

The bewitching hour when the moon rises and the owl hoots had arrived. It was time to rumble.

But we had locked him in for the night and he had to vent his wild side within the 28-foot walls of a travel trailer at the Crosseyed Cricket Campground.

Canoe shows a certain amount of discretion, even when he feels rowdy. He seems to know that he has to play quietly because we're sleeping, but there are times when exuberance exceeds the bounds of propriety. With us in bed and him running around, we can only imagine what he'll find as play things.

When our eyes closed and our minds wandered off, Canoe found the stopper in the bathtub and exclaimed, "IT'S TIME TO PLAY HOCKEY!"

He slapped the stopper around as if it was a puck – off the side walls, into the corner, a body check against the side of the litter box, back toward the drain, HE SCORED! Now, a word from our sponsor.

When a guy sweats, he needs a strong deodorant. Hi, I'm Dwayne Schlotsky, and I use Purge. Purge leaves me fresh, even when I'm out on the ice. And you can imagine how much the other hockey players appreciate a guy who smells like lilacs. Even my dog likes it.

"We're back with you for this second quarter of play between Canoe and the four walls of tub in the trailer. The trailer is losing and Canoe showed remarkable skill in this first half. Let's see what he'll do in the second.

"It's the face off. Canoe has the puck. He's rounding the far corner of the tub, over the blue line, slapping, swiping. The puck is flying. Canoe is mid air. He catches the puck in his teeth, wheels, lets loose and bats the puck against the fiberglass as he works it down toward the drain. The crowd is going wild. (We're sitting up in bed, wondering what's going on.) …And the shot…IT'S IN THE LITTER BOX!

"It was headed for the drain, then it hit the corner, popped up and ricocheted off the faucet and landed in the litter box. Canoe has to go into the 'sand trap' and pitch it into the end zone. (Pause.) Now he's in the box, he's scratching, he's digging…he's turning around and using his hind legs to pitch it out! It's up, it's flying, crap is flying, everything is flying. You can't tell a puck from muck. Where's the puck? There it is, it's falling…. IT'S IN THE SOAP DISH!

"Canoe leaps against the wall trying to dislodge it. He's got it, swatting, swerving. He's going for the Cat Trick; he does it. IT'S IN FOR ANOTHER GOAL. CANOE: 2, TUB: 0."

When I turned the light on in the washroom, Canoe was in a tub that looked like a desert in a windstorm. He was smiling, his eyes were big and black, his tail was swishing and he had an impish look.

"What?"

Chapter 10

Mischief With Ethics

Every shelf in the trailer was a challenge for Canoe. He walked the shelves above the stove where the spices lived. He walked the shelf above the dinette where mail was stacked, and over the bed where bedtime books and reading glasses lay.

Walking around and amid all the obstacles required balance and stealth, but should his body brush them, they'd come tumbling down onto the bed…and us. "Sorry, folks, I didn't mean it." Always this feigned innocence.

A cat that used to run with other cats and small kids finds that life with two ripening adults is boring. He has to find his own fun.

You would not think that a Q-Tip is much of a plaything, but to a cat it's a baton. It has a hairy end that sticks to his barbed tongue like Velcro and he can be acrobatic and carnival. It flips; he bounds, twists, spins and scrambles. It's the ultimate accommodating toy for the mellow oldies who like it quiet. It's like watching television with the sound off.

In the morning, there is a new arrangement to the things that you left on the shelves at night. Watches are under the bed; glasses are on the floor; Q-tips are everywhere and the old newspapers that were stacked at the door ready to be discarded, are strewn about. Computer discs have been rearranged in catful artistry, which is no artistry at all.

In the morning he'll be standing on our chests, looking down, his little nose against ours. He always prefers Eva to the scratchy old guy. He'll purr his wake up call, slide his face along hers and lay his head in the bend of her neck and give lots of licky kisses. Licking a guy may feel like another Q-tip surface, so Eva gets all of the kisses. Isn't this the way it always is?

If we continue to sleep, he'll be off the bed, on the bed, bounding off and on and over the bed like a phantom. We'll catch images of him air borne over us. He'll pounce on a moving foot as if it were a forest mouse. He'll find a hand that moves and make it the object of his affection or his aggression. He bites, which we can interpret as cute, bothersome, confrontational or damn irritating. To him, it's a hard kiss.

He discovered that he could crawl under the comforter between the layers of blankets and along the labyrinthine contours of our legs and bodies. He crawls in the dark cotton subway to the opening near our heads, emerging with a smile. Of course, cats don't smile, but he has this message in the dilation of his pupils and the studied silence of his stare as he waits for the next act of devilment.

It's amazing to see the rambunctiousness of a hunting carnivore with the brakes on. It's mischief with ethics. He rarely goes beyond the edge of cute or appropriate behavior, although there is a strong signal from him. "Sleep is over. Get up and feed me or play with me."

I think cats bring life to a family where kids used to provide the stimulus. They keep play in our lives and substitute mischief for the seriousness that overtakes our lives. It's childhood revisited. They don't care about finances and responsibility and deadlines. Life is a lark. It's how we could live again.

Chapter 11

She's on the Floor Again

Eva has laser-sharp concentration on tasks before her. The world is out; the task at hand is in. There is a serious hunkering down attitude when she's working on something, and for several weeks it was the construction of the new house and the publishing of our boating book. The trailer was strewn with files and photos, construction plans and roof samples. Eva, the editor/publisher, struggled with details and deadlines. Unfortunately, this is a task for a certain kind of mind, which Canoe and I don't have.

When an onerous task becomes burdensome a person needs an escape to something pleasurable and enjoyable. A rhapsodic experience will do. The cerebral needs to be shut down and the carnal limbic system turned on. You know what I'm referring to. You need to play with a cat.

There is a noticeable difference in Eva's disposition when the cat is around. Canoe doesn't understand pressure and deadlines. He knows about simple pleasures, about cuddling and playing, so he goes over to Eva and expects to make love to her. She's distracted for awhile, but he persists, and he sits on her lap or nibbles at her papers. You can see her giving way, first annoyed, then amused, then delighted. On the wings of a cat she's lifted off the carpet and away from work and into the realm of play.

Simple pleasures occupy too little of our time. We don't make love enough. We don't sit idly in the sun enough. We don't listen to music — really listen to music — or stop the car and watch Holsteins wallow in a farm pond. We don't shut off our world of care and performance, and just be.

Time with Canoe is time to play. You can't really do anything else. You can't cook and play with the cat, write with the cat on your lap, talk to each other when the cat's the center of attention.

Canoe is our meditation, our therapy. Eva would be a different person without him. I like her this way. When she grooms him, he's grooming her. His warm body and fur coat fill her with pleasure. He lies on his back with his legs splayed while she untangles knots of fur and talks to him. He licks his paws in a kind of mutual grooming exercise and both of them smile.

She talks to him like a mother talks to a child on the changing table. A cat never gets beyond this infantile stage. He remains soft, needing care and being solicitous and affectionate.

I wouldn't go so far as to call a cat in the house, marriage counseling, but our house is more peaceful with a cat in it, and my wife is happier with two males in her life.

Chapter 12

The World Is His Carpet

There isn't a place in the world that cats don't think is theirs to lie upon, to walk upon, to play upon. This includes human chests, stomachs and heads. It's preposterous that a cat has this temerity, this self- assurance, this kind of audacity. Who does he think he is? What makes him think he can walk on us at 4:14 a.m. and not get whacked?

You'd think he would use a little discretion — walk only on the hard parts, do not walk on the tummy or private areas. Never walk on a nose. He is so sure of his place that he's surprised when we move him.

The kitchen counters, the table, the skinny rail along the walls in the camper, the hood of the car, the top of the boat, the computer keyboard — all are his lair, his place to play and observe the world.

I'm going to put a stop to this. Unbridled liberty leads to a lack of control and a disregard for authority, and the next thing you know your cat will be downtown playing pool with the other cats. Tomorrow there will be new rules on walking.

"Is that okay, Canoe?"

Chapter 13

Canoe, You're As Dumb As A Fish.

In our cove on the lake where our house was being built some big bass get caught time and again. Tournament fishermen take Bob the Big Dumb Bass to the scales week after week and release him. He goes back to his haunts in Raven Cove and eats little fishes and darts after anything that moves — things like silver spoons with flaming red tendrils, green plastic snotty-looking things, stuff that looks like cheap costume jewelry, anything that dances and flashes. A fisherman in a bass boat entices Big Dumb Bob to bite one more time, and he never disappoints. He goes to the scales, again, and everybody oohs and ahs, and he feels a little embarrassed, but, hey, he's a fish.

Cats are a notch above this. One of the most inventive things ever created for cats is a fishing "lure", actually a couple of strips of real hide (probably rabbit) tied to an elastic cord and a rod of green plastic with a suction cup. You place this fishing setup on a mirror, on a door or on your forehead and go fishing with your cat.

You can also troll this saliva spattered fur piece in front of your cat and he'll look at it with the same killer instinct that a real mouse evokes. He'll pounce, you'll pull away; he'll crouch, you'll dance your fish/mouse seductively around his body and he'll go crazy. He's wired for this; the hunter part is right next to the play part so he doesn't know the difference. He spins and snaps until he's got it.

When we're away for a few hours we know he's been fishing because his "lure" will be in a new state of death with the leather chewed and the fur wet and torn. Obviously, it doesn't have to be on a pole or a string or have motion. He'll give life to it if it has none of its own. Canoe will flip on his virtual reality helmet and see a live beast, even though it has only a vestige of real life. A patch of skin, a scrap of fur, a set of beady eyes sewn onto a sliver of hide is sufficient to get the killer instincts going.

It was early one morning. The squirrels weren't yet running through the trees and Eva was deep in her neverland when we felt the soft pads of Canoe making his way across the bed. I put my hand outside the cover and he buried his head in my hands, giving himself a facial massage while I fondled him.

Then he walked across my chest and went to Eva, her face buried in linens with an inviting nostril and corner of the mouth available to Canoe for kissing. His scratchy tongue moved over her nose and in the corners of her mouth. She rolled over to face her tormentor, muttering affectionate sounds, which Canoe took to mean, "You love me. Okay, I'll give you more."

This brought on further giggles and the impulse to make love to a cat or to run away from this rough tongue with germs and microbes from other cats, garbage, squirrels, crickets and who knows what else.

After a giggle fit and some head moves that discouraged his licking, Canoe went to the floor alongside the bed and came back to the top of the bed. That's when we heard the ZZZZZIIIIP... SPLAT sound. We couldn't figure out what he was up to until we saw that he had brought his fishing pole into the bedroom and the pole was caught beneath the bed and he was pulling his "guppy" onto the covers. With tension from the elastic cord, his "fish" wanted to get away; so as soon as he lightened his grip, the thing would zing across the covers and smack the wall. He'd retrieve it, bring it back on the bed and release it again with another ZZZIIIPPP... SPLAT.

  This went on until his attention waned, which is close to the time a three year-old kid tolerates fishing. Now I'm sitting at the computer typing this in my underwear before I take a shower and he's thinking about jumping onto my lap. "Don't even think about it, Canoe. Nooo, pleeeze...,YEEEEOOOOOOOOOW!"

Chapter 14

The Hunters Come

We saw a big pickup pull into the campground loaded with cut wood. The driver stopped across from our campsite and began unloading. Four huge logs formed a square with cut wood piled in the center. His trailer, full of additional wood, was pulled to the side and separated from the truck.

Soon other men arrived, pulling an assortment of pop up and travel trailers. Surrounding campsites filled and soon there were hunter-orange hats and vests all over the landscape along with back slaps, boisterous laughs and loud talk. It was the opening day of deer hunting season and there was going to be a lot of male bonding going on at the Crosseyed Cricket Campground.

Canoe watched all of this from atop the computer, and when it came time for him to go out, he went straight for the burly men and the pickups and the pile of wood that was now smoking and coming to life as fire. Five men totaling a couple-ton of he-man bulk stood face to face with the smoky fire as a six-pound pussycat strolled among their legs and looked up.

"Hey, pussycat. What do you want?" one man scowled.

"Just thought I'd hang out with you guys," Canoe said in

his little boy voice.

"Get lost, pussycat, or you may end up in the fire."

"You mean you're not going to let me stand around here and do a little male bonding with you guys?"

"How about a drop kick into the fire, pussycat?"

Canoe went from man to man, but a hunter with a can of beer in his hands, standing around a fire with a bunch of his buddies ready for a rowdy weekend is dispositionally eons away from being friends with a stray cat.

"But I'm not a stray cat," Canoe seemed to say. "I'm cute and cuddly and I got a soft belly. Wanna feel?"

"Yeah, I can feel it now. Right on the tip of my Army boots. Scram, you mangy alley cat!"

"I am not an alley cat. I live right over there in that trailer. Be nice. I just want to hang around with you guys."

Canoe sincerely believed he was a lover and could win over even the toughest hunter, the coldest heart, the most callous criminal. Canoe picked out a young man in the company of older men and began another conversation. "I didn't want anyone to get mad at me. I just wanted to say, 'Hello, and welcome to the neighborhood.' "

The young guy looked at Canoe, stooped down and stroked him.

"I knew it," Canoe mused. "There is a softy here. Now I've got to work on the others."

Every man, woman and child was the potential for an affectionate relationship with Canoe; so he stayed around, rolled over in the dirt next to the fire, and finally walked off slowly to smell a tire and examine their tents and motorhomes.

Then we heard Goliath, The Hunter, holler, "Get out of

there, CAT." Eva hurried out the door to retrieve Canoe who was climbing the canvas of a tent. The hunter apologized to Eva for his harsh treatment of Canoe as she picked him up and took him home, holding him cheek to cheek to console him.

But Canoe was not adequately chagrined, not sufficiently rebuked, scolded or threatened, and the next chance he got he was back in the camp of the killers for another smell, another look, another conversation with the guys who had slaughter on their minds.

In the waning light, when men and cats prowl, there was stuff going on around the fire that only a cat can relate to. Canoe was in the shadows listening to the kind of talk that happens only around beer and fire.

Canoe said to himself, "I wonder if his wife knows he talks this way. Boy, if I could tell the wives the things I heard, I'd be able to blackmail these guys and make a fortune.

"And the belching! I've never heard belching like that before. I wonder if those sounds are in the can, or do they make them up. They can keep talking with belches built right in."

"So dis guy's in a Lincoln, driving along like he's half-dead… *(BELCH)* ...and I come up in the Ram… *(BELCH)*… and I flash him with the roof lights and he gets all … *(BELCH)* …nervous and pulls off on the side… *(BELCH)*… of the road and lets me… *(BELCH, SWIG, BELCH)*…by. Boy, he was filling his pants… *(BELCH, SWIG, SWIG, BELCH)*."

Canoe came home that night smelling of smoke, beer and external body fluids which men around campfires are known to produce. In the morning the hunters were off for the big hunt, leaving a smoldering fire and beer cans strewn about.

And we think cats are animals.

Chapter 15

We're living with a Schizophrenic

Like the prodigal son who thought that life beyond his father's realm was where the action was, Canoe spent hours looking out the window. His favorite perches were atop the computer and on the nightstand beside the bed. He represented the pioneering spirit in many of us who look beyond home, marriage and job for a personal journey. Somewhere along the pilgrim path, we secretly yearn to throw off the shackles and go wild.

Many times in those first weeks Canoe seemed to walk between his old life at the singlewide and his new life with us. As often as not he would be gone when we wanted to go to bed. We'd go outside and call him and sometimes go looking for him in the dark woods, but many times we'd just give up and go to bed. On those occasions we'd be in bed with eyes wide open, like we used to when a teenage kid was still out. We tuned in to sounds in the woods and any hint of Canoe's bleating meow. We would have torn off the blankets and ran to the door if we heard him, but all was quiet and cold in the campground of the Crosseyed Cricket.

We talked about how wild animals seek shelter on bone-chilling nights. Maybe they find a cave in the rocks, or beneath a giant tree that fell during a storm. House basements and trailer crawl spaces can be a roof over their heads. We got up periodically to check if he was waiting on the steps of the trailer.

When he finally came home, he immediately went to his food dish and chowed down. Finishing, he looked at us with a strange and bewildering look. Neither strokes nor cuddles or baby talk could erase a far away look. He was distant, his pupils dilated, his body language aloof. We followed him with our eyes, trying to reestablish the relationship.

He seemed to be deep inside himself or in some far-off place where he spent a lot of his time. A curtain dropped around him and we knew there was no way we could reattach to him.

Sometime later Canoe the cuddler came back. Out of his sleep emerged the lover cat we knew and by morning Canoe had fully returned. He kissed me on the mouth, then the nose. His purr was loud and it made me smile. I couldn't sleep any longer with him sitting on me and staring into my face. I rolled him off and he attached himself to Eva, loving her so intently she awoke giggling, then annoyed. He persisted, pushing his face into her neck and nibbling. This cat knew how to make love.

Then like the click of a switch he changed to fighter. Gone was the lover boy. Now we had the scrambler, the biter, the clutcher, the tumbler. He was cycling through his personalities: Canoe the wild animal, Canoe the lover, Canoe the scrappy windup toy. What are you, Canoe? You're schizophrenic.

Chapter 16

Lo, How A Rose N'er Blooming

There comes a time in a male cat's life when he passes from pussyness to catness, a transition between childhood and adulthood; the passage from the sweet innocence of soft underbelly and cuddly toys to the serious business of carousing, peeing on posts and scratching everything in sight.

This turning point is the bar mitzvah of the feline kingdom, the Ritual of Responsibility, a time when human custodians and friends of animals take their cats by the paw, look deep into their eyes and announce, "It's time..., time to meet with the surgeon at the PPAW (People Protecting Animal Welfare) Spay and Neuter Clinic, big guy."

We bought a cat carrier for the occasion, a transportable house with peek-a-boo slats where he could observe the world around him, yet feel snug in a den with four walls and a dark green towel laced with catnip. He liked it.

The morning of the ceremony saw Canoe rising at the appointed time, which was way before the human population arose in the fifth-wheel trailer in the woods; but there was a sadness in his nips. Gone was the early morning exuberance that found him licking our faces, crawling under the covers, walking, nay running, the ledges that held glasses, canisters of film, screws from Ron's pockets, loose change and chapstick. This morning was going to be his wedding day (in reverse) and there was a melancholy jaunt in his step, a sadness of leaving behind forever the ways of his youth and thoughts of wild escapades with feminine felines and broods of kittens looking like the old man.

We put him in his carrier with the catnip and the green towel and his favorite tennis ball. He loved that tennis ball. Wherever he was, the tennis ball was there too. The ride through the Tennessee countryside brought us to Greenback and the PPAW Clinic. Big Mac was there to meet us, a beefy cat who was picked up at the local McDonalds where he had spent a lifetime begging scraps from hamburger lovers. Fattened and fortified with hundreds of quarter pounders and chicken nuggets, Big Mac had become the clinic's resident greeter. He sat on a ledge of the receptionist's desk eyeing newcomers, unmoved by hysterical animals about to lose their sexuality.

We said our good-byes through the slats of Canoe's portable den and brought him to the back room for the *Ritual of Responsibility*. We assured him it wouldn't hurt.

"You can pick him up after 4 pm. By that time he should be able to walk a straight line," the clerk said.

Late in the afternoon we carried Canoe out in his carrier. He meowed in recognition as we talked to him and took him to the car. Back home in the fifth-wheel trailer, Canoe seemed to be half the cat that we had brought to the clinic in the morning. He walked like someone who had his spunk removed.

Canoe could have been the Daddy to a lot of little kayaks and canoes but we didn't want any homeless animals dumped on the side of the road. Now we think that there should be spay and neuter clinics for despots and shrill politicians and some radio talk show hosts whose voices need to be mild meows.

Canoe enjoys his first snowfall in the woods.

Chapter 17

Hide and Seek

When Canoe is ready to play Hide and Seek, he's jazzed. He crouches in delicious anticipation. His head twitches, his tail swishes, his driving (rear) legs get planted and he bounds toward us, attacks, then runs off in a wacky giggle. Sometimes we don't know we're playing the game until he jumps out at us from behind a wall or a piece of furniture. Then the game begins in earnest.

But he doesn't realize you're supposed to do it on an alternate basis, so we have to be patient and run around a lot. Sometimes he's always the hider and we're always the seeker. When found he runs off to hide again. Sometimes if we hide, he forgets the rules and goes to sleep or grooms himself. Meanwhile you're hiding and your spouse comes into the room and finds you behind the bed and he/she wonders what you're doing there. You feel a little foolish, only to discover that the two of them play the same game when they think you're not looking.

We become absolutely adolescent with a cat who plays without baggage or apology. Cats are innocent and straightforward. They do things without thought as to whether it's proper or stupid or sophisticated or if anybody is looking. If they've got to lick their genitals, they go for it. If they want to swipe a blind, they swipe. If they want to bound out of the chair, or onto the chair, or around the chair and over the chair, they do it. If they want to sleep on someone's lap, they jump up and settle in. If you're working on a project, they plant themselves on top of it. They think not of consequences or propriety.

Hurray for the crazy cat.

Canoe sharpens his claws on the handle while playing in a basket.

Chapter 18

Travels with Canoe

It was a dark and stormy day, and we had miles to go before we slept. Our first stop was Indiana, then Chicago, then on to South Dakota for Christmas. The temperatures were nearly balmy when we left Tennessee, but an Arctic cold front was moving down and before it, rain was falling. This was a near guarantee that we would see rain turn to sleet, freezing rain and snow.

We had taken Canoe on short trips to see how he traveled. He didn't seem to have a lot of anxieties on those short trips, but a long trip of over a thousand miles was full of uncertainty. We brought the pet carrier lined with the fluffy green towel, put a litter box on the floor of the back seat, packed water and food and hoped for the best. The carrier would be his safe place, his asylum.

For the first hundred miles of each day, he was uncomfortable, pacing, looking at the fast moving world around him, occasionally squealing quietly, a low, back in the throat complaint, but otherwise tolerating it. He'd test his carrier, pulling the blankets over his head and find some solace in his plastic den.

The first stop was Cousin Martin's place, a rural home on the Indiana prairie. We arrived as a sleet storm threatened to drive us off the road. Coming into a home was heaven for Canoe. He surveyed the inside perimeter of the house and crouched under every bed and piece of furniture, gathering dust bunnies and smacking lost buttons and runaway bottle caps. Bo, the big Chesapeake lab, was moved to the basement and Canoe had the run of the place. His plastic egg, which we had taken from home, became his hockey puck on Martin's hardwood floors and he played a solitary game with no goals but a lot of body checks against the doors and cabinets as padded feet and claws lost traction on Martin's waxed floors.

The second day of travel to Chicago Canoe had moments of restlessness, wandering the length of the car from the back window, across the backs of the front seat and across our laps. He'd stand with his front paws on the steering wheel, looking around, catching images of overhead bridges, then trying to get onto the dashboard of the car, which he quickly learned was off limits.

When we arrived in Chicago at the Useltons, a short day's drive from Indiana, there were two animals to greet him – Sandy, the big yellow lab, and Cleo, another tuxedo cat. Cleo was a kindred kind but not a kindred spirit. Losing her territory to another cat provoked hisses and suspicion. Canoe, in his innocence, was sure she wouldn't mind if he ate from her bowl and crapped in her litter box.

Cleo also was replaced by Canoe for granddaughter Zoe's affections which probably didn't help Cleo's disposition. Zoe picked up Canoe and dressed him in doll's clothes. Canoe didn't mind looking like a stuffed animal at a Cracker Barrel Restaurant and we slobbered over him and Zoe and made Cleo feel like yesterday's worn out toy.

Cleo was never at peace as long as Canoe was there, and Canoe explored far and wide and never was intimidated by her. It's difficult to take a cat with positive self-esteem and put him down.

Sandy was another thing. Sandy was the size of a small pony and her wet nose and penetrating stares bore holes through Canoe. Sandy stood like a Field and Stream model, one front leg raised and cocked, eyes ahead, head still, tail straight out, long nose quivering.

This hunting posture was no consolation to a six-pound cat, so Canoe's little paws made flicking jabs toward the immobile yellow lab. Sandy backed up in surprise as Canoe jabbed and parried. Sandy didn't understand. She wanted to play. She wagged her tail, approached again, waited, flinched, wagged her tail and approached again. The lightweight pussycat was a flurry of jabs and fancy dancing; the heavy weight stood flat-footed wondering what this was all about. At round five, nobody was ahead and neither opponent had touched the other.

It was measured distance between hostility and friendship. The relationship was warming about the time we had to leave for a long day's drive to South Dakota to sister Lelia's.

Lelia's house is a 1900's house of many dimensions, rooms,

hallways, closets and a dirt basement, all of which were in various stages of remodeling following a fire. This is junkyard heaven for a cat and for hours Canoe was lost in the confusion of the big house on Third Avenue. What was not dusted before, became dusted by Canoe, and he nonchalantly wore a thin film of drywall dust, sawdust, lint and dead bugs. He looked LeMiserable but he was happy.

We had the upstairs bedroom at Lelia's, and thought that Canoe would follow us to bed and sleep at our feet; but Canoe never came to bed, and even in the morning's early light there was no cat beside us. It turned out that Canoe slept with Lelia. Unattached as he was, unattached as she was, he saw nothing strange about sharing Lelia's bed. Not only did he share the bed, he snuggled beneath the covers where their two bodies shared the beat and heat of life. So warm, so supple and so beguiling was this in-law body, that Canoe couldn't separate himself from her. Eventually, as Lelia left her warmed linens, Canoe wandered upstairs to us. There wasn't a hint of remorse, not a smidgen of regret, not an iota of guilt, not a look that begged for forgiveness.

"So, this is what cats are made of," I huffed.

He seemed to hear, and began licking Eva around her face and lips until she giggled and welcomed him back and forgave him for his waywardness.

"You're just like all men, Canoe."

Chapter 19

Cats are Like Children

The temperature was diving for zero and a dark ominous sky forecast cold and blustery weather for Mitchell, South Dakota. It was a perfect and fitting setting for Christmas Eve as we donned down jackets and headed for church. But just before we left, we discovered that Canoe was in the earthy basement of Lelia's Victorian home with the stack stone foundation and dirt floor and boxes stacked on pallets.

Among the rubble and the clutter were boxes of D'Con to control the rats and mice. In Canoe's explorations, he knocked over a package and the blue granules poured onto the floor. D'Con is edible; ask any dead rat. Canoe discovered that too. Lelia found him with his face in the stuff, but we didn't know if or how much he'd eaten. This discovery took place as we were about to go out the door. What to do? We decided to go to church, sing carols and pray.

On our return Canoe was given a cocktail of vitamins and a ground-up capsule of bioflavinate which we thought contained Vitamin K, a substance that promotes blood clotting and might negate D'Con's effect of induced internal bleeding.

We learned later that bioflavinate is vitamin P, which probably helped Canoe's P but didn't do anything for his K. In the end, we didn't do much for him except to cuddle him more and worry.

He was fine. Cats are like children, getting into everything and being totally irresponsible… and resilient.

Canoe plays with Christmas tree ornaments at Lelia's house.

Chapter 20

"There Were Ninety and Nine That Safely Lay..."

There were ninety and nine that safely lay
In the shelter of the fold.
But one was out on the hills away,
Far from the gates of gold.
Away on the mountains wild and bare;
Away from the tender shepherd's care.
(*The Ninety and Nine* by Elizabeth C. Clephane)

Back in Tennessee it was like a summer day, high in the seventies in February, the middle of winter. But a cold front was due to sweep through during the night, dropping temperatures and bringing cracking and booming of thunderstorms we had forgotten about while living in California.

Canoe was glad to be home at the Crosseyed Cricket Campground after spending a day with us getting the new house ready. When he jumped out of the truck, we knew that after eating he'd make contact with that Feline Netherland where cats hang out and carouse at pubs and turn over garbage cans; but somehow we didn't want to curtail his adventurous side by keeping him indoors.

We made supper, gave Canoe his rations along with fresh chicken from our meal, and he was gone. The weather worsened with wind howling through the trees. By bedtime the temperature was dropping rapidly, and Canoe was still not home. This was happening too frequently. We were torn between giving him his freedom and keeping him confined to the trailer. What would we do when we moved to the new house?

I fell into bed by 10:15 and was gone. Eva came to bed at 11:15. Still no Canoe. Each time there was a vibration in the trailer, one of us went to the door. Maybe it was Canoe jumping up on the metal step.

At 1:00 a.m. I got up and opened the door to see if Canoe was home. Obviously he was spending the night in the company of others. Cats? People? He was such a lover, anyone could open their door and he'd be in their lives.

Or he could be in the company of the wild cats of the underworld. Heavens knows where that leads — wild women, unhealthy food, neighborhood bars, pool-shooting cats, cats in fast cars. Then there are communicable diseases and pests — mites, ticks, fleas and other biting varmints.

At 4 a.m. I went to the door, turned the light on and stood in the doorway like scrooge on Christmas morning, homely with sleep, motionless in the yellow light of the trailer's outdoor light, staring into the darkness. I gently called, "Canoe, are you out there? Come home."

The wild winds whistled around me and into the trailer. The expected rain had not yet arrived but the messengers of bad weather shook the trees, sending twigs onto the roof.

I left the light on and went back to bed. Cats don't need a night light, but if the prodigal son needed a beacon, he'd have it.

Eva asked if he was home. I mumbled that he wasn't. We slept restlessly.

This was a *cat* we were fretting about. After seven kids, you'd think that a lousy cat was not up to this kind of concern. We were both surprised with our fretting and sweating. We were losing sleep over this animal. Rain began to fall. We dropped the overhead hatch and closed the louvered windows.

By 6:30 a.m. Eva was up and at the door…and Canoe was there, dry, sitting on the upper step, unconcerned. He was cool; we were upset. I heard Eva greet him.

"WHERE WERE YOU, YOU LITTLE BRAT?" (She's mad and she's letting him have it. Canoe sidewinds around her legs.)

"I missed you." (But she loves him and she's really happy he's home.)

"DON'T YOU REALIZE YOU HAD US UP HALF THE NIGHT WORRYING ABOUT YOU? WE DIDN'T KNOW IF YOU HAD BEEN HIT BY A CAR, TAKEN IN BY SOME CAMPERS WE DON'T KNOW…OR AN OWL COULD HAVE EATEN YOU… OR YOU GOT CAUGHT IN A TREE…OR FALLEN AND BROKEN A LEG AND YOU'D BE LYING ON THE GROUND GETTING WET AND YOUR BODY TEMPERATURE DROPPING AND WE'D BE FIFTY YARDS AWAY, LYING IN BED WORRYING AND WANTING TO FIND YOU, BUT NOT KNOWING WHERE YOU ARE. DON'T YOU THINK ABOUT THESE THINGS?" (She's ticked-off and the jugulars are bursting, but Canoe continues to sidewind around her legs.)

"Do you want some food?" (She's calming down and melting with compassion.)

"YOU KNOW, I'M NOT GOING TO LET YOU OUT AGAIN IF YOU KEEP THIS UP!" (She's not through yet. Canoe stops sidewinding and looks up at her wonderingly.)

"Now what kind of Friskies would you like? The seafood platter or the chicken livers and giblets?" (She can't wait to give way to romance.)

"AND ONE MORE THING: YOU CAN'T JUST COME HOME AND EXPECT TO BE TAKEN IN AND FED LIKE EVERYTHING IS ALL-RIGHT!" (One last tirade. Canoe watches her prepare his food, licks and stares.)

"There how's that? I'm so glad you're home." *(*She's broken down. When will she ever learn?)

"YOU BRAT!" (Ah, one last denouncement, but she doesn't mean it. She's got tears in her voice because she cares so much and she's so glad to see him. Canoe is deep into his food and he's not catching a word.)

I holler from the bed, "WHERE IS RIGHTEOUS INDIGNATION? SINCE WHEN DO WE TOLERATE AND WINK AT PHILANDERING AND WASTEFUL LIVING?"

Rain fell, the windows steamed up and we all went back to bed. The lost sheep returned, the shepherds slept and everything was quiet in the trailer in the woods where there lived a man and a woman and a cat called Canoe.

> *"…All through the mountains, thunder riven*
> *And up from the rocky steep*
> *There arose a glad cry to the gates of heav'n*
> *Rejoice, I have found my sheep."*

Chapter 21

Canoe Makes the Move to the New House

He stayed under the bed in the new house as workmen ran through the house fixing lights, attaching heater vents, painting trim. There was too much house for Canoe to comprehend. After his existence with us in a space measuring 8 feet wide by 28 feet long, he was in a strange new world – 30 feet by 50 feet with two stories, a staircase, closets, counters to run across, large windows to the woods to look through, and the lake and all those strange people.

But play overcame fear and after a while the clutter of moving and packing materials provided endless possibilities for recreation. Cats, we learned again, despite their careful deportment and meticulous personal care, are really junkyard dogs in cat coats. They love junk, and the more artistic – that is to say, mindless, formless and random – the junk is, the more they like it. A new house being moved into must be like the garbage around the cans in the city. The scene is always changing, the scents are ever new, and the places for mice and men and cats are endless. Every blind corner is intriguing. Any open box, half-filled box or box filled with packing material is fascinating and must be explored.

The jumble of discarded boxes in the garage became cat heaven. No inventor could design a playground as deliciously chaotic as the rubble of moving. Canoe loved the rustle of plastic, the spongy transparency of bubble wrap and the infinite underground paths through the boxes. But even cats are creatures of habit and established routes began to develop through the debris. We'd see him surface, take a look at us and dive back into his world of stuff, exiting from the tunnel to Neverland at a predictable point. We'd greet him again, call to him; he'd turn and dive back under and come up where we expected to see him.

And that's the way cats live – foraging, discovering, uncovering, reaching out until the territory is known. And if it changes, like it does in the garage of a moving family, so much the better. It's simply new territory, new worlds to explore.

He especially liked a large transparent bag full of plastic peanuts. He buried himself in "ghost poop", scratching, looking out to us through a film that resembled water glass on a shower door.

But Canoe's playground was our given task. The object for us was to make the rubble disappear.

In a week the house was orderly and Canoe's playthings went into the dumpster or the fireplace. Right now he's looking at me and thinking, "Let's move again. That was fun."

Chapter 22

Of Mites and Men

It was the old classic. Man finds cat. Cat has mites. Man has mites. Man has BITES. Man ITCHES. Man claws at red spots that drive him crazy. Man blames cat.

(Cat looks up, knowing he's been accused.) Cat says, "Who, me? They're not biting me. Look at my belly. Do you see any varmints?"

Man says, "I know where you get these things."

"Yeah, where?"

"From all the carousing around you do."

"I do just the normal amount of cat carousing. Maybe it's your relatives."

"Pardon me. What do our relatives have to do with this?"

"When we went to Indiana and stayed with your cousin Martin and his big clumsy dog and the chickens and the cows and his cats. Maybe they had it and handed it off to me."

"Well, maybe. But you didn't have to go under the beds and play with all the dust bunnies."

"Hey, dust bunnies are animals too. I was in that car for 12 hours. I was going nuts. I had to have something to play with."

"It wasn't 12 hours; it was only 8. Still you had no business being Martin's cleaning cat. You could have sat like an angel and simply enjoyed our evening together."

"You don't want a cat. You want a door stop."

"Oh, quit it."

"Or maybe it was the Useltons, and Sandy, their slobbering yellow lab. That dog would not leave me alone. What's with him? Is he some kind of pervert?"

"He was just interested in you. I like Sandy. Don't put him down."

"Or Cleo, their fat tuxedo cat who looks like a distant relative. She could have given me something."

"C'mon. She was perfectly groomed and very lady-like. And you violated her. You used her litter box and ate from her bowl."

"She didn't care. She didn't have the energy to care. Boy, is she dull!"

"Stop it. She doesn't have your alley cat savoir vivre, but I thought she was very nice. And she behaved like a house cat should."

"Nice? She's half-dead? Did you ever see her go faster than 2 mph?"

"You're unkind. Both Sandy the lab and Cleo the cat were cleaner than you and spend a lifetime at home minding pillows and carpeting. They don't have your personal habit of visiting every hole in the wall and playing in the woods with anything that moves. Besides, what were we to do? Leave you home?"

"These are your raylahtives, and I had no choice in the matter."

"Quit talking like a hillbilly."

"And let's not forget Lelia's big house in South Dakota, the one with the dirt basement that went to Neverland, and the upstairs rooms with tons of remodeling debris and dust as thick as my coat. I HAD to play in it. I was captive and you wouldn't let me go outside. What's a cat to do when you're downstairs listening to Christmas music and drinking wassail and playing games with Lelia's boyfriends? How many boyfriends were there, anyway? I lost track after the third night. Three nights, three different guys. Whew. I don't know how she does it."

"I think you're getting out of hand; show a little respect. That's Eva's sister you're talking about."

"Yeah, she was cool. In fact, I slept with her."

"We know. You'd sleep with anybody."

"She's bigger and softer than Eva. You ought to try it some-time, Ron."

"You're impertinent."

"Well, I'm sure someone who smells as good as she does, does *not* have bugs, but they could have come from her *house*. I think you've got to remember that before you plucked me out of the woods at the Crosseyed Cricket Campground where you were living like a couple GYPSIES..."

"Gypsies? We were living on the fly while our house was being built. Watch your tongue."

"...I was the picture of health. Neither mites or ticks nor any varmints were on me."

"Pardon me. You were housing a passel of fleas when we found you, and you didn't even know it."

"But I was cute and friendly."

"Now you're arrogant and haughty."

(Cat rolls over, looks up meekly.) "I'm sorry for being a

pain in the patoot, but I didn't ask for this pestilence of red itching dots you and the lady are experiencing."

"We'll deal with it. You'll just have to have a bath. "

(Cat jumps up like he's been electrocuted, and stares at the man. His eyes are flared and his ears down, ready for battle.) "A BATH. NO. PLEASE. NOT A BATH!"

"Oh, quit being a baby. Maybe we'll rub you down with this white medicated solution that smells like crankcase oil and then we'll smoke the house."

(Cat thinks this is far better than a bath.) "Whatever. I take my fate stoically."

So we got this stuff with skull and crossbones on the cover — E-RADICATE —, designed to snuff fleas, ticks and lice. There wasn't any mention of mites, but we assume that something so vile, so medicinal and so toxic smelling would kill anything. Maybe even the pussycat; but we had to take the chance. The bottle said it was safe for cats and that their coats would be lustrous and soft, so we weren't worried.

Canoe got his toxic rubdown with two humanoids holding his paws, switching between consoling language and scolds, until he was wet and stinky and despicable. He was so disgusting that no one loved him, except the mother, who loves anything small and sick.

And we treated the house with BUG OUT, which we sprinkled around, swept in and vacuumed up. The house wore a thin film of toxic dust, which was all around and up our noses and left us with the fear that our mucus membranes were going south.

But the bites stopped, and so did the itching and the red spots. We were becoming normal again.

Canoe, however, continued to look like a junkyard cat days after the treatment. His coat was oily and streaked and sticky to the touch. He was awful. So we decided he needed a shower.

(Cat overhears the conversation between man and wife and becomes alarmed. Uptight. Anal, even.) "A SHOWER? CATS DON'T DO SHOWERS. WHAT BOOK ARE YOU READING? I DON'T TAKE SHOWERS. I DON'T TAKE BATHS. I HATE WATER."

"Look, a little water never hurt a cat. We'll do it very gently and it'll be over before you know it. Don't get hysterical."

"I'M NOT HYSTERICAL, BUT THIS IS MY LIFE YOU'RE DEALING WITH. WE CATS HAVE EONS OF WATER HATRED BEHIND US. AND THERE'S A REASON FOR IT."

"Oh yeah? What might that be?"

"IT MESSES UP OUR MINDS. IT SCREWS UP OUR HAIR-DOS. IT DISCOMBOBULATES OUR BOWELS. IT MAKES US LOOK SILLY…AND IT JUST AIN'T RIGHT."

"We'll talk about it later. Calm down."

Chapter 23

Thou Shalt Not Bathe A Cat

Cats have rules:

1. Don't even think about bathing me. I do that myself, thank you very much, and any interference with this natural process borders on insanity.

2. Water is for drinking. Period. Okay, gold fish can swim in it, and cats may on occasion pluck fish from water, but we don't swim in it. We don't swim with fish. We don't swim with nothin'.

3. Fluids over two-inches deep have weird and ominous properties, and any cat in his right mind will not get his paws near it nor his mouth, unless it's milk.

4. Wet stuff is flicked off our paws because it has no place on our bodies.

5. Showers are cool for humans because humans stink. Cats don't. Have you ever smelled a cat with BO? I don't think so.

6. Cat lick is like mother's milk. It never stinks, cleans anything and is *the* universal solvent. That's as wet as we want to get.

Deaf to the mutterings of our cat, however, we observed that the automatic cat cleaning mechanism was not getting the job done. So I reasoned, "If the cat takes a shower with me, and I place the shower wand on the floor so there is no water falling from above, and if I'm in there with the cat and the warm water is flowing and I hum *Love's Old Sweet Song*, then maybe...

1. Canoe would go ballistic and I'd be in the shower with a clawed and fanged jungle animal that is climbing up and over my naked body which would become a mass of bloody scratches. The cat's claws would rip across my face and snag my eyes until they hung from their sockets like balls on strings. For the rest of my life I'd be scarred, eyeless and ugly. I would be so contemptible that my wife would leave me, and the cat would be gone too, because she would take him with her, and I'd be wifeless and catless and I wouldn't even be able to find my TV dinners.

Or...

2. I would kneel down and pin the cat with my knees and my left hand while handling the shower wand and the shampoo and the hairbrush with my right hand. I would massage and work the shampoo into his fur, under his chin, between his legs and around his ears. Then I'd try to rinse him and would spin around chasing him with the shower wand. He'd use me like a ladder and be over the top of the shower stall, and still sudsy and sticky, he'd go tearing through the house and I'd be after him streaking naked and wild-eyed. I'd corner him and he'd launch himself onto the piano slipping and sliding...

Or...

3. I would take a totally humanistic approach and move softly and sympathetically, knowing that, to a cat, water is vile. And I'd take the cat in my arms and we'd let the water flow over

our bodies together, and I'd make soft murmurings to the cat and he'd get showered, and I'd get showered and we'd be friends forever. (This is the hopelessly romantic ideal scenario.)

These things and others I imagined as I lay in bed with Canoe next to me, trying to develop a game plan for cleaning him. Question was — how much force, how much love, how much tact and understanding was necessary? I figured every angle.

I got out of bed, took fresh clothes to the bathroom, and returned to the bed where Canoe lay looking at me. Could he read my mind? Do I pick him up now and go to the shower with him? I returned to the shower, began the water, put the shower wand on the floor so that only a small fountain of water cascaded up six inches and fell gracefully down. It looked non-threatening to me. I went back for Canoe, then chickened out and returned to the bathroom alone. But just before entering the shower, I saw Canoe still looking at me which I took as a divine message, so I went back, picked him up, and entered the glass shower stall with him in my arms. We stood there. So far I still had skin and two eyes.

I set Canoe down on the wet floor with the spray from the shower wand wetting the floor and his feet. He did not go ballistic. I waited. I wet his paws. He did not go ballistic. He wasn't happy either, but he wasn't out of control. His pupils were dilated and his ears were back, but he was still sane and reasonable. I took shampoo and began massaging his legs. He did not go ballistic. He began to circle like a cow in an auction ring, looking for the door. I pursued, slowly, talking softly and humming an old Moravian hymn. Gradually and continually I shampooed his legs, then his back, his belly, his shoulders. Foam and water splashed around his pretty little face. I washed him until he was a fraction of himself, a drowned kitty who had lost 15 pounds simply in the process of getting wet.

He was still and passive. I rinsed him, shut off the water, rubbed him with a big towel, hugged him, kissed him, told him he was terrific, and released him. He ran to the living room to undo with his tongue what I had disarranged with the towel; then he went to Eva, who was still in bed. She consoled him, toweled him some more and took him beneath the covers to warm him and assuage his anxiety and trembling. Finally he was dry,

his pupils small, his ears up and his fur soft and supple. He was beautiful. He got hugs and kisses and for the rest of the day enjoyed new popularity.

Funny, how a well-groomed cat is more lovable than a cat that looks like he's been hanging out at auto graveyards. Now if we could just stop him from showing curiosity for the underside of the truck and car.

Chapter 24

Paper, Paper, Get Your Early Morning Paper

We've all had phases in our lives when we were fascinated with certain things. Little girls have a doll phase, little boys their wooden soldier phase, men go through a motorcycle or a guitar phase. Canoe is going through a paper phase.

There was a lot of paper with moving. Canoe particularly liked the triple-layered paper that protects mirrors and pictures. It retained its original shape when it was un-wrapped so it made heaps and towers of paper with narrow alleys and side roads that provided him hours of discovery. He was having so much fun with them, we left them on the living room floor for days.

Paper walls reflect heat, and any warm enclosed space is ideal for taking a nap. We'd look for him and he'd be nowhere around, but when we began un-peeling the pile, there he was, sleepy-eyed and lazy, wondering what we wanted.

Toilet paper also was amusing to Canoe. One day Canoe went into the bathroom and swiped at the roll, which obligingly unrolled, leaving a trail of paper which he first tasted, then felt. Then he swiped again. Anything with motion or sound has life, so he swatted it again and again until he got it up to speed, and paper rolled off in piles on the floor. We caught him lying in a puddle of Charmin. He really looked cute.

But re-rolling toilet paper is tedious and a bother, and after a while it ain't so cute. When we're in bed and I hear the toilet paper roll unrolling, I'll scream and run into the bathroom and he'll run out. I'll spend fifteen minutes trying to make it look like a roll on the wall again.

I've thrown pillows, books and any missile I can get my hands on when he does this; but he's catching on, he knows how short my fuse is. He'll start; I'll sit up, reach for grenades; he'll dart out of the bathroom; I'll wing my objects, and he'll giggle all the way to the kitchen where I'll find him at the food tray as innocent as a monk.

We've gotten to a point where a loud "NO!" stops him, but that also has the effect of scaring Eva half to death because this usually happens around 6 a.m. We're happy he hasn't found much pleasure in the morning newspaper. If he gets to reading and playing with Garfield or Bucky, we'll be in for some additional mayhem.

Chapter 25

Teetering on the Edge of the Porcelain Canyon

Water has life to a cat. It refuses to be grasped, disappears into things, drops from the sky, runs across the ground and is gone. To a cat, water is about as interesting as a running mouse. At the same time, water evokes terror in a cat. What is the most terrible thing to a cat is also the most fascinating.

Canoe's latest find is the "flush toilet." Canoe considers this magic. Water comes from nowhere and with the click of a handle comes up and around and down a hole. And then the little pond fills again. To a cat, this is more miraculous than a walk on the moon.

Canoe's curiosity has gotten to a level that if we perch on the seat of "Waterworld," he waits and looks between our legs, behind the bowl, in back of the seat, circling around again waiting for a view. This is a bit of an intrusion. An animal watching you in your most private moment makes the music stop. You don't know what a cat thinks. Does he understand shame and nakedness? Does he gape when you drop your pants and look with astonishment at something that you (and your wife) consider very ordinary? Does he giggle or have any thoughts about flab, paunches or rolling contours?

If we should rise before the swirling stops, Canoe perches on the seat, his head deep into the bowl. If we want to please him, we flush again. But toi-let seats do not provide a good claw-hold for a cat, so teetering on the edge of the porcelain canyon is perilous. On several occasions the cantilevered cat has gone over the edge and into the pot. Then there's a lot of sloshing about as he tries to plant his feet on a slippery slope with rushing water dragging him down; but quicker than we can imag-ine he catapults out of the pot, flicking his paws as if

he had just touched something awful.

For a cat, the toilet has to rank right up there in excitement with scurrying mice and fluttering moths.

Chapter 26

Breaking Out

Since Canoe had retained his primitive ways, he always wanted to be outside. We'd only been in our new house in the woods a short time and thought it best to keep him confined for a few weeks before allowing him to venture into unfamiliar woods. We had seen other cats and wild animals and didn't want him to get hurt or forget where home was. We didn't know if he'd stay around the house or if he'd try to seek his feline playmate far away at the Crosseyed Cricket Campground.

On a few occasions when a door was opened, he made a break for the crack and got outside, and I took off after him. It became a spectacle that stopped people in their tracks – Canoe racing up the 200 foot-long driveway with his ears pinned back, his body low (so we couldn't see him) and me running behind in stocking feet or house slippers or in my underwear, calling, "C'mere, Canoe, Canoe, Canoe, Canoe, CANoe, CANOE, CA-NOE! CANOE!!"

One morning workmen who were stuccoing the foundation of the house stood motionless, stucco dripping from their tools as they watched me running up the hill hollering, "Canoe."

They looked to the water, then back to the cat. "This guy's a little confused," they thought.

Canoe got to the top of the hill, turned into a briar patch, then started back down the slope through the woods toward the house. He slinked in the brush close to the house where I caught up with him, blood in my eyes, socks worn thin, my irrational self saying, "Strangle him," my reasonable self saying, "Don't hurt him or he'll quickly learn that, 'C'mere Canoe,' means pain and suffering."

So I picked him up by the nape of the neck, the parental mode of correction, put him in my arms (with a full Nelson hold), and brought him back to the house, talking softly to him through gritted teeth.

Often his escape resulted in *The Mother* standing on the upper deck, yelling, "He went that way," and me in hot pursuit, crashing through the woods with the cat nimbly bounding through the trees ahead of me. He'd escape to a neighbor's home where he'd bound up the deck stairs. I'd follow until he was cornered. The only way for him to escape was vaulting over the railing to the ground twenty-feet below or give up. That's when I would grab him and take him home.

After he was acclimated to the neighborhood we wanted him to be able to come and go as he pleased, so we installed two Cat Flaps – one from the downstairs into the garage and one from the garage to the outside.

Teaching a cat to walk through a closed door requires a little thought and planning. The Cat Flaps were transparent so Canoe could look into the garage. Cats have experience with glass and they know they can't walk through it, but this glass door was hinged, and no glass door or window that Canoe ever encountered was hinged.

He had to push it open with a paw, insert his face into the crack and tolerate the tactile pressure of the swinging door on his head and across his back. The final challenge was the nipping of his tail as the door swung down and squeezed the tip.

Eva went into the garage and swung the flap in and out while Canoe was in the house looking at her crouched on the garage floor calling, "Here, kitty, kitty," while peering through a tiny glass door. You can imagine he was wondering if she didn't have anything better to do. In a few minutes, Canoe pawed the door, making it move. He pawed at the top of the door, however, where the hinge was. He needed to push on the bottom.

Within fifteen minutes Canoe had it figured out. All the moves were tentative, but after a day of pawing and experimenting, he got the glass kitty door to move, then placed his face against it, let the door slide up over his head and across his body until he was through the opening. The critical part seemed to be his head and shoulders. If the head and whiskers say it's okay, the dumb part tags along.

Now we had a new problem. If we opened the garage door without making sure the inside Cat Flap was locked, Canoe bolted through the cat door into the garage and was outside before the door came down. We weren't ready for him to have the run of the outdoors yet, so the chase began again.

We were new to the neighborhood, and people were beginning to talk. Raising Canoe was turning out to be a public affair and I was gaining a reputation as a mad man who roared through the trees in pursuit of a black and white blur hollering, "Canoe."

Chapter 27

It's Time To Put On The Training Wheels

There comes a time in a cat's life when Dad says, "It's time to put the training wheels on, son."

It was four weeks since we moved into the new house, and I decided it was time. I did this of course, while the mother was still in bed. The day was warm and dry and I thought, "I'm going to let Canoe outside and see what he does. He's had time to examine the woods from windows in the house. I don't think he'll wander off."

He had two kitty doors to negotiate: one from the house into the garage and the second one from the garage to the outside deck. To date we had only opened the one from the house into the garage.

I released the latch on the garage-to-outside kitty flap and waited outside. Canoe seemed to be saying, "You're kidding, aren't you? That door has never been opened to me before. You're going to let me leave, then you're going to carry on like a crazy man again, aren't you?"

I swung the little glass door back and forth, giving Canoe a sense of reality. He pawed tentatively, then purposefully, then pushed his head through. He was standing on the deck, and I was at his feet (neither in stocking feet nor slippers, but fully clothed, with hiking boots if I had to bushwhack to find him), and I wasn't screaming or threatening or scolding.

Canoe moved tentatively along the deck to the stairs at the west end, then slowly went down to the big tree stumps where he sharpened his claws. It felt good to be outside. He looked and looked and looked. He cast a glance back toward the house where I stood, still cool, still in control, still permissive, muttering consoling and comforting nonsense, "I'll be here for you when you need me, son. Just have a nice walk and come back. I'll be waiting and together we'll have a glass of wine, light a candle, listen to piano music and have a pleasant evening."

Canoe moved to another log where he surveyed his kingdom better. He again glanced back to the house where I stood, then crept down the slope toward a giant, fallen shagbark hickory tree. Its limbs reached up and out like a cadaver in rigor mortis. It was a perfect Jungle Gym for Canoe He walked through its limbs, down the entire trunk of the tree, stopping for a moment, listening to a bird, crouching. He had lost sense of me or the house. He was free.

You could sense that the bond that we had was lost. He had transcended into another sphere. It was heartwarming, to see him in a natural setting, living the adventures of a free animal. He wasn't knocking over anything that we owned or unrolling toilet paper or doing anything in our household where his behavior threatened our order.

He moved off the big shagbark hickory and tentatively walked the forest floor. It was soft and crunchy. He walked as if he was trying to be quiet, each paw settling down only after tentatively feeling the surface in a stuttering movement. He came to an outcropping of rock, stood for a moment and looked around, then went down into a cleft of the rock where he disappeared.

I went inside and watched his movement from an upstairs window, accepting whatever was going to take place, but ready to follow if he moved out of our territory and beyond my vision.

Mother Eva came onto the scene, fresh from her morning shower, and asked what was going on. I told her Canoe was on his own. She looked a bit worried and said, "Well, it has been a month. Where is he now?"

Together we spotted him. He was coming back up the big shagbark hickory, rubbing his mouth on small limbs, listening to the sounds of birds and wind in the trees. Eva stepped outside and called, "Hey, Canoe, are you having a nice walk in the woods?"

Canoe stopped, looked, and instantly bounded off the shagbark hickory, across the crunchy forest floor and onto the deck where she greeted him and they each nuzzled the other.

He escaped the grasp of wildness and willfully moved back into the confines of our domicile. We tried the training wheels, and hey, he already knew how to ride.

Chapter 28

A Cat With Dirty Boots Leaves his Signature Everywhere

With both doors opened to Canoe, he moved freely from the house to the garage and from the garage to the outdoors anytime during the day. When he awoke in the morning, we'd let him out and he'd go down to the big shagbark hickory log or head toward the cove.

He'd come back in from his early morning patrol by the time I was having breakfast. I'd set his food out, he'd go back out and make the woods his litter box, then bop in and out of the house throughout the day.

We often sensed that he became a little more distant emotionally from us when he spent a lot of time outdoors. Bad weather kept Canoe inside. His choice. He'd look through his little portals, ponder the situation and say, "Nah, I'm not going out today."

But if the rain stopped, he was outside, which created another problem. A cat with wet feet is like a guy with muddy boots. You could follow his footsteps and see exactly where he had been.

Keeping him off the kitchen counters has always been an

objective. We don't like the cat licking pork chops or nibbling the coffeecake. Whenever I caught Canoe on the counter, I'd scream such a hideous scream, I'd wake the dead or startle Eva to such a degree that she'd scream. Each time Canoe would jump down and run from my terror.

It was very ineffective. If I was in the room, Canoe would show his remorse by immediately running away, sometimes retreating to the dark and cold of the garage where he'd sit in silence. I'd open the door and find him looking at me. He'd stay there for a half-hour, then come up as if there was no kitchen incident.

"My sins are forgiven, I know it. Maybe I don't have any sins. Counter tops. What counter tops? I can't remember walking on any countertops. You didn't want me to walk the countertops? Okay, I won't do it anymore. Anymore is right now, right?"

This kind of thinking drove me nuts. Because he had the run of the outside now, and because it was wet and muddy, he'd tell me exactly where he had been. And I didn't like what I saw — dirty paw marks across the kitchen counters, across our bedside tables, the dresser, the window sills, the top of the car, the desk, the computer. The only place where pussy paws could not be found were on the ceiling.

So I said to the Mom, who incidentally won't let me inside the house until my hooves have been inspected and cleaned and I have switched from my work boots to my slippers, "Mom, I think when its raining and muddy, we lock the outside kitty door. The cat can go into the garage, but he can't go outside until it dries out some."

I got her opinion on how I should have placed straw on all

of the exposed muddy surfaces around the new house, even though tractors continue to put in steps and walkways and any straw I'd put down would be covered by mud again the next time workmen came around.

Canoe heard this conversation, and the next morning at 5:43 a.m., when people sleep but cats and roosters rise, he was standing on my chest, looking at me with big eyes, pleading silently for freedom. He had to go. He didn't want to use that despicable litter box again, and would I please let him out. "PLEEEZE."

I rolled over. "Go away. It's only 5:43 a.m."

He went into the kitchen and knocked over a glass. "HE KNOWS HE'S NOT SUPPOSED TO BE ON THE COUNTERS," I screamed silently to myself, trying not to wake myself or be disturbed. "I think he does this for spite. I'm not getting up."

I hope spring comes soon and ground cover hides the raw earth. In the meantime, I had better go for a load of straw. The woman and the cat are in alliance.

Chapter 29

Don't Hurt The Cat, You Bully

Cats don't learn some lessons easily. When spring came, the air was full of bugs. First wasps, then June bugs. These were wonderful playmates for Canoe and we'd see him outside jumping and twisting to swat a flying varmint.

He liked the position next to my side of the bed that looked over the driveway. From there he had long looks into the woods, to the house next door and up the drive. And this was a good place to swat wandering insects. Before the screens went up on the new house, he'd sit there and lean out, nearly falling a story down to the pavement below, but because he had most of his weight in his rear end, he was able to teeter, without falling. As soon as the window screens went up, his leaning stopped at the screen and any bug that was curious about the impish feline face on the other side could do a "Nyah, nyah, nyaaah." This would drive Canoe mad, so he'd swat the dumb thing and they'd feel his smack and fall to the pavement or restart their engines half-way down.

This bug swatting business began at daylight. As soon as there was anything in the air or on the screen, he was scratching at it or swatting it. This does not prolong the life of a screen and disrupts the sweet early morning sleep of the man of the house. Besides, the man of the house does not relish replacing the screen at the hardware store because there is a tear in it. So every time this animal started his pre-dawn swatting and scratching at the screen, the man would awake himself and his wife and half the county, with a Neanderthal cry, "No, NO, NO, NOOOOOOO." Of course, by the time the last echo – O O O O – was bouncing off the walls, Canoe was scampering down the hall, giggling. He'd always get away without me swatting him. By the time I'd raise my pillow, intended to be a mortar round, he was gone.

I thought that the threat of my justice would teach him, but I could never touch him. My raised pillow or my first guttural cry was enough to send him running; but he'd be back in two minutes as though the threat meant nothing at all. I took this as insult. Morning after morning, my best sleep (where the luscious blond walks over to me and says, "Hey, big guy, wanna fool around?") was disturbed by Canoe scratching and swatting the screen.

Usually I stretch before getting out of my bed. One morning when Canoe scratched at the screen, I went ballistic, swinging at him and chasing him through the house, down the stairs, around the vehicles in the garage, into the spare bedroom, into the bath, through the other guest bedroom, into the under-the-stairs storage area and back into the garage. If I could have caught him, I would have strangled him. I picked up a yardstick along the way and swung violently. I poked every corner and swept viciously under every bed.

Content to think I had scared the living hell out of him, I returned upstairs, tired, panting, mad and with a yardstick in my hand that was flaming red. I had turned an ordinary household item into a red-hot poker.

At the top of the stairs I heard Eva in the kitchen…with Canoe. Somewhere in my sweep through the downstairs he had evaded me and gone back upstairs while I was fuming and venting and chasing some other cat. Now he was sitting puckishly on the kitchen floor, looking sweet and innocent and not even hiding behind the mother's skirt. He shouldn't be so sure.

Of course, I cooled down. It didn't have anything to do with Eva saying, "You're not going to hurt this cat, are you, you big bully? He's only a cat. Cat's are curious. Cats love to chase bugs and look out windows, blah, blah, blah, blah." Must have lasted two hours. I showered.

Now he's brushing against me while I sit at the computer. He probably knows I nearly killed him this morning.

He wants to go out. Okay, I'll go downstairs and open his kitty door. He follows, awaiting the moment when he can go wild and chase bugs and jump and pirouette. I open the latch and the kitty door, show him it's open by swinging it to and fro. He looks, DOES NOT EXIT, then goes back upstairs with me and is winding through my legs.

What am I going to do? He loves me.

Chapter 30

The Loss of Innocence

Canoe approaches every new cat that roams through the territory with innocence and openness. But he's learning that cats, like people, come in an array of characters.

There are lover cats who brush up against you and ask to be stroked; they want a relationship. There are comfortable cats like Big Mac at the vet's office; they remind you of sales people at Sears, pleasant but inconsequential. There are narcissistic cats, beautiful but dumb. They love being adored but don't give much back.

There are political cats that give you a smiling meow, then crap in your flower box. You can't trust them, and you don't want them as your friends. There are worker cats who have a worried look. They're into country western music, hard work, poor pay, bad bosses and lost girls. They're harmless but you get tired of hearing about their sorry ass lives.

Then there are underground cats, cats with character deficiencies and mental disorders. They spit venom and they'd sooner bite than talk. Their mission in life is to intimidate and beat up other cats. They've never learned how to look sweet on the mantle or take soothing strokes from a passerby.

In the first month of freedom while living in our new house on the lake, Canoe found two feline associates. Unfortunately, neither of them turned out to be playmates, which was Canoe's sincere desire inasmuch as he left behind at the Crosseyed Cricket the little gray short hair that was his buddy. There were moments when Eva would look at Canoe and say, "Hey, big guy, are you depressed? Are you missing your little friend at the Crosseyed Cricket?" Then Eva would turn to me and recall how she'd find Canoe bursting through the woods with the little gray cat in pursuit. It was feline heaven, two cats with each other and the woods, two lively kids nearby in the trailer, full food dishes and loving adult campers all around. Then we came along, adopted him and took him away from his familiar surroundings.

Canoe's first encounter at the new house was with a black Manx who sauntered across the property. The Manx was far from home on his excursion, and he probably assumed he bought the territory, because when Canoe walked up to him and introduced himself, Canoe got a raised back instead. Canoe found this strange; he only wanted to be friends. But the message was clear; so Canoe worked his way gingerly back toward the house, which the Manx interpreted as defeat and retreat, and pursued, and soon there was a squabble with the Manx following Canoe into the garage through the kitty door. When we heard the squabble we went to the garage and saw the Manx scoot into the privacy of the truck's undercarriage where he perched above the rear axle. Canoe moved in tight to observe him. Fear had not yet taken over and curiosity was still in place. We tried to coax the Manx out of place using Canoe's hopeful optimism, but sweet talk got us nowhere. I opened the garage door, started the truck, and backed up. The Manx shot out like a ball of soot, up the driveway and out of our lives. It was a long time before we saw him again.

The encounter with an orange tabby was more dramatic. There was a fracas downstairs and Eva rushed to investigate. In the garage stood a lean orange cat with guilt and guile in his eyes. He quickly exited through the open garage door and onto the rear deck where Eva again encountered him. For a moment it appeared that he might be friendly and she tried to talk kindly to him. He moved away, afraid and skittish. A soft voice filled with consideration was not comprehensible. He hesitated, then moved quickly off the deck and into the woods.

Canoe was nowhere to be found. Eva called, "Kitty, kitty, kitty, where are you, Canoe?" No response. Eva noticed a brown streak on the kitty door. She touched it, then smelled it. Feces. This was an extraordinary circumstance. She checked the nearby litter box, but there wasn't a trail of fecal evidence there.

She went upstairs and began telling me what she observed. "I don't know where Canoe is," she said. Minutes later Canoe crept up the staircase, cautious and wide-eyed. Eva picked him up and noticed fecal material on his fur. His anus and sides, and even the top of his back were streaked. She began a more earnest examination. A right rear toenail was missing and bleeding. A puncture wound appeared in the upper back thigh and another one lower down. Canoe was sensitive to the touches and winced as the mother examined his body. She turned him sideways and upside down until there was a full scrutiny of his body.

"I need to give Canoe a bath," Eva said. "Can you help?"

I started the water in the shower while Eva cradled Canoe and entered barefoot into the shower with him. Soothing words and gentle massaging followed. Canoe circled uncomfortably with Eva in slow pursuit, shampooing, rinsing, talking softly and concluding by massaging him with two big towels.

We dressed the wounds with antibiotics and set him free. He was walking with a limp. The mother examined him again, rotating him like a pig on a spit until she uncovered more puncture wounds further up on his back and rear end.

We figured this is what probably happened: Canoe had gone out to greet the orange cat. The orange cat stood and grimaced. Canoe looked surprised. "I thought we could be friends," he signaled.

"Get lost, pussy cat."

"Look, I don't want any trouble. You can walk across our property anytime you wish."

"Why don't you disappear, pussy cat. Wherever I walk people and pussycats get out of my way. The world is my hunting ground, and you're in it. Scram."

"Okay, I'll go back inside. Don't bite me."

For a cat with the Devil in his heart, the visage of a competitor retreating is as delicious as rare salmon. The terrorist attacked Canoe who by this time was in full retreat, his ears down, his hind limbs galloping in giant strides, and the orange monster catching up and pouncing, sending his fangs and claws into Canoes hind legs and thigh. As soon as Canoe could get himself upright again, he was running, through the big garage door into the garage. Canoe's eyes were wide with terror, his bowels a storm of chaotic impulses. The orange cat pursued him, catching Canoe as he tried to negotiate the kitty door into the house. Wounded and fouled, Canoe charged through the door, his feces marking the kitty door, with the orange menace glaring from the other side. Canoe retreated under the bed in the downstairs guest room and awaited the next assault.

That's when Eva heard the ruckus and went downstairs to investigate.

By nightfall, Canoe could hardly walk. His rear end was swollen and we wondered about bowel punctures and infections from the foul-mouthed cat. We named the orange cat Slobodan because it appeared his goal was to ethnically cleanse the neighborhood of other cats. I went to bed around 10 p.m. but at 11:30 Eva was standing in the beam of the hallway light, asking me to help her give Canoe a slug of oral antibiotic left from his neuter surgery. I got up; she held Canoe and talked to him while I positioned the eyedropper in the corner of his mouth. He opened, swallowed and we stared at each other. This was too much like scenes from family life with kids. The same parental instincts, the same juices, the same intensity, the depth of caring were coming to play. Canoe, warm and helpless, cradled in Eva's arms, accepted it like a helpless child.

She took Canoe downstairs, close to his litter box so he wouldn't have to walk the staircase if his soreness and stiffness increased. He settled in uncomfortably in the room near his last encounter with the orange tabby.

By 6 a.m. Eva was creeping downstairs to see how her baby was doing. He looked up at her and muttered a weak, bleating meow. He hadn't moved. She brought the water and food to him and he drank and drank. "Take it easy, little guy, you're going to burst if you drink too much." She removed the water from him temporarily, then moved it back again and he drank more.

Later in the morning I walked downstairs to see how our

guy was doing. He mouthed a sweet reply, stood up, stretched, started toward me, then stopped, and sunk into his original position, favoring the wounded thigh.

Two hours later Canoe had moved from the floor to a chair where he had a better view of the lower deck and any possible visitors. He was able to jump from the floor to the chair. Eva came down again and we discussed his situation.

I thought Canoe would be fine, but mothers leave less to chance and take the more compassionate route. "Ron, we've at least got to go to the vet and get some more antibiotic. I don't want to take any chances on an abscess developing."

Workmen were to arrive at the house that morning, so I awaited their appearance instead of accompanying Eva with Canoe. "She's going to be upset if they choose to keep him for a few days of observation," I thought.

The vet shaved the affected areas, treated the puncture wounds and examined the missing toenail site. He gave Canoe a shot and some oral antibiotic with instructions for dosage and care. Canoe was going to be fine. He was sore and stiff for a few days but soon was his normal, frisky self.

Chapter 31

The Scourge Continues

Two weeks after the encounter with Slobodan, the scourge of the countryside, we were out for the evening and upon entering the house looked for our greeter. Oftentimes Canoe heard the garage door open and greeted us at the downstairs door. But he was nowhere to be found, so we brought in our things and started to prepare for bed.

But the mother doesn't rest easily when her children aren't home so she went for a walk through the upper level of the house, occasionally calling out from the upper deck. Then she went downstairs and found him lying on the rug. "There you are, Canoe. How come you didn't come and greet us?"

She went to him and started to scoop him up into her arms. He hissed, snapped and cringed. "What's wrong, sweetie?" she cooed.

Then she saw his bloody backside. In an alarmed voice she called, "Ron, he's down here and he's hurt."

By the time I started moving in her direction, she was coming up the stairs with Canoe, wide-eyed, catatonic, disheveled and motionless. Apparently, while we were out, Canoe was also out, not learning his lesson that wild cats in the neighborhood are territorial and rule as far as they patrol. Slobodan, or another terrorist, took umbrage with a tuxedo cat exploring the catnip grove.

Canoe was too sore to move, and he unresistingly gave into Eva who began another examination of his bloody body. Puncture wounds and a world of litter covered his hind legs and rear end again. Canoe doesn't like showers, but this situation required that the three of us to get into the shower. We shed our clothes down to our underwear and began the exploration of Canoe's matted hair and bloody body as warm water poured over him. We bathed him, dried him, administered first aid (patch, repair and antibiotic), second aid (comfort and soothing words) and third aid (warm milk, vitamins and a soft bed) and put him downstairs near food and his litter box. Then we went to bed. I went to sleep. Eva stayed awake, staring at the ceiling and worrying.

In the morning he was better, moving slowly, but he was moving on his own. He even tried to jump onto his favorite perches, such as the side table to the sofa, but he was sore and stiff. He missed his mark and fell back, surprised at his own ineptitude.

Continuing with the antibiotic, he was better the following day, and on the third day he had his natural curiosity back and playfulness resumed. When he walked across the bed and gave me his morning licks, I knew he was cured. He was not running, but he was able to jump onto chairs and resume most of his activities, including roaming the territory within a 500 feet radius of the house. We decided to lock him in the house earlier in the evening.

Eva went to get the mail that afternoon, up the driveway on the street. Alongside the road and about 200 feet away was Canoe, oblivious to the threats that wounded him only a few days earlier. Eva trundled him home, warning him of the perils of wild cats and the fact that with two wounded legs, he had no legs to escape on. She kept up the lecture, telling him he should be a house kitty, that it was dangerous out there, that he had everything he needed inside — soft food, hard food, warm milk, classical music, birds at the feeder to watch, soft beds and a chair of his own.

"When will you ever learn?" This of course went in one fuzzy ear and out the other.

We began to restrict his outdoor time to daylight only and bring him in before dark. We tried to keep him close to the house, away from the street and cars, although he already had a healthy fear of engines noises.

Besides Slobodan, there was the little black Manx and two others we'd seen, a tabby Manx and a long tailed calico cat. None of them were going to take to kindly to the presence of Canoe.

We supposed that Slobodan was an unaltered male cat. Canoe, on the other hand, was a gelding – a neutered male – who lost whatever aggressiveness he had. Canoe was like a panda in a cage of tigers.

It wasn't more than a few days after Canoe's last mauling and he was missing in action again. By now we knew that Canoe had a special attraction for a woodland lair up near the street. Eva went looking for him and while calling his name, heard a meow from the woods. She peered through the trees, and 35 feet away was Slobodan looking at her and meowing. But what startled her even more was Canoe, huddled in a thicket of tall grass closer by, but not responding to her call at all.

As Eva approached Canoe, he did not leave the security of his lair, but rather stayed hidden, silently maintaining his position. It was as though he was saying, "Shh, don't tell him where I am." He was motionless and frozen in place, paralyzed with fear. Eva walked past him toward Slobodan who came toward her, apparently in a friendly disposition. Eva bent down to talk with him knowing he was the killer, but surprised to find him receptive to a compassionate hand. She reached out to touch him, talking to him, but he backed off, turned and ran a few feet away. She turned and went to the place where Canoe lay hidden and picked him up. Slobodan again came out to the street and Eva approached him with Canoe in her arms. Canoe was very agitated by this confrontation and attempted to claw his way out of her grasp, urinating down her jeans.

Eva walked the long drive back to the house with Canoe in her arms. He was terrified and motionless; his pupils were dilated and his ears were laid back. I was working in the back yard and she found me and told me of the encounter.

"I wish we could catch him," I said. "I'd hit him with something and kill him."

"Well, here's your chance. He followed us down the driveway," she said.

Eva again confronted Slobodan with Canoe in her arms. Again Canoe attempted to escape from her. There was no doubt that Canoe was pointing the finger at the cat that was terrorizing him. Slobodan now stood a few feet away, acting almost friendly, but Canoe looked through the facade of domesticity to a cat that had eradication on his mind.

Eva put Canoe inside and locked him in the house, returning to continue her "friendship" with Slobodan. Meanwhile I picked up a short handled hoe that I thought I could drive through the skull of the thug. Eva enticed Slobodan close to her and petted him. He curled around her like a genuine pussycat. Was he a cat with some chance of rehabilitation? We wondered. Maybe he was abandoned and was doing his best to find food and stake out a territory. Canoe, in contrast, was comfortable in his home and care and guaranteed love and affection. But what could we do to secure Canoe's life and be humane to a creature that responded to affection?

We decided that if we could get him into the carrier we used for Canoe when traveling, we could either kill him or bring him to animal welfare. Maybe we could have the veterinarian euthanize him (okay, kill him) and we'd be finished with the traumatizing period.

Slobodan moved away from Eva as I approached with the cat carrier. I had a can of cat food and tried to entice him in, but he was suspicious. I stopped my advance and Eva followed Slobodan a few feet into the woods, calling softly, "Here, kitty, kitty." He came back to her and she picked him up by the neck and hindquarters – gingerly holding him out at arm's length so she could drop him if he got wild. She carried him to the driveway where I waited by the carrier baited with a can of cat food. As Eva approached the carrier with Slobodan he began writhing to the point where Eva couldn't contain him so I grabbed him by the neck, forced him to the ground and shoved him in the carrier. The carrier rocked with the motion of a tiger in a tank. We struggled with the door clasps and stood by to examine our quarry. Now what do we do with him?

Chapter 32

What To Do With Slobodan

The urge to kill Slobodan passed. I imagined all the scenarios where I would take his life. I'd fasten a rock to the carrier and lower it like a casket into the lake with Slobodan inside. I could see the bubbles emerge as Slobodan writhed, gasped, struggled, urinated, defecated and suffocated. I couldn't bear the thought.

I imagined putting Slobodan by the exhaust pipe of the truck, close the garage and make a homemade gas chamber. But I was short on the killer side.

Maybe I could take him out and strike him across the head with a hammer. That would be quick.

The more I thought about the ways of murder, the more I softened. A call to the local veterinary clinic revealed that it would cost us $17 to have him euthanized. Somewhere in our compassionate selves, we wanted another opinion. I called a neighbor, an animal rights person with contacts in the county for stray animal control. She suggested I take him to Loudon County Animal Welfare.

"Ramona will assess Slobodan and determine whether he

is adoptable," she said. This felt better. Ramona would make the decision, to die or to live. If she thought he ought to be put to sleep, it would be her decision. We would be free of the guilt and there would be no cost.

The only criteria I had for Slobodan's new life was that it was not to be lived around here. Any cat with a criminal record like his, no matter how you justify it on the basis of survival, had no business being left loose again; and we weren't sure how domesticated Slobodan could become.

In the morning I put him in the trunk for a ride in the country. I didn't hear Slobodan wail as we went down the road. Maybe he liked it; maybe he was traumatized; maybe the bluegrass and rhythm and blues was drowning out his sorrow.

I walked into Animal Welfare swinging Slobodan from the carrier. Inside two friendly black cats greeted us. They were not put out with Slobodan, or me, or a foul smelling carrier. They didn't have any horrific experiences with the scourge of Timberlake Drive, so why should they? Still I thought that a wide-eyed cat peering through the slats of a carrier would evoke some response from them. They seemed to own the place, occupying as cats do all the prominent positions — top of the desk, next to the phone, by an ash tray full of butts. Dana came out and we talked for a moment before Ramona arrived.

"Are you Ramona?" I asked. She looked surprised.

"Okay, what have I done?" she replied smilingly.

"I've heard about you, Ramona."

"I hope it's good."

"It's good. You're going to help us make a decision about Slobodan. He's been bad, terrorizing the neighborhood, sending our cat to the veterinarian with hip and rear end punctures, and generally being a pain. Maybe he should be snuffed; maybe he should be given another chance. It's going to be your call."

"Let's have a look," she said. She took the carrier and walked into a room full of cages and animals. This had to be a situation strange and offensive to Slobodan. Cages of cats and none to kill or mame. With the door closed she coaxed Slobodan out of the pet carrier and into the animal welfare cages where he had fresh litter, food and water. I was impressed with the institutional cleanliness that was ten notches up from the wildness and uncertainty of his life in the woods along Timberlake Drive.

After a few minutes she came out and said, "Snip, snip. I think we can save him. We'll deprive him of his manhood and that may take the fight out of him. He was not hostile to me and welcomed my strokes. He may make a good housecat."

"Only if he doesn't come back into our neighborhood, Ramona. I don't think I can trust Slobodan, testes or no testes."

Whether or not Slobodan made it in another place with a loving family was to be seen. In the meantime, Slobodan would live in a wire cage, with no balls at all, wondering if he would have it as good as Canoe. We hoped he would. He's one of God's little ones who had it tough.

As I drove away, I thought of Dana and Ramona and all the angels of mercy. They are not socialites or the beautiful people. They're not money; they don't shop at Saks and never appear on the social pages with their lawyer husbands who contribute a wad for visible social causes. They are the plain people, who work next to the recycling yard. They dispense affection, consideration and respect for the lost and found.

On second thought, they are the beautiful people.

Chapter 33

Cat Neverland
It's Right up There with Heaven, Hell and UFOs

Slobodan's capture was followed by a period in which Canoe was a model household cat. He was affectionate, never strayed further than the driveway and usually went outside only when we did.

But gradually, his memory of the marmalade mauler left and he began to wander again. Mother Eva was particularly put out with the fickle fondness he had for us, his on-again, off-again attachment, and before bed she would make sure he was inside. Sometimes this required a walk up our long, steep driveway to the paved street above.

Canoe was often found walking the woods and the grounds across the road near Harry and Jane's, but he would usually respond to her coddling calls of "Kitty, Kitty" and come to her. She'd stumble down the drive with the cat in her arms, mumbling to him about his waywardness, how much she missed him and his ungratefulness for a good home.

One night Eva was up late doing her nails and watching television, which has the value of nail clippings, so I went off to bed. Eva called me back and asked if I would get Canoe.

I walked the street, going toward North Cove, a half-block away. It was one of those warm nights with mild breezes when cats and teenage boys hate to come home. I walked the road calling, "Canoe, Canoe, Canoe," hoping neighbors wouldn't hear me, yet calling loudly enough to evoke a response. I came back the same way, then went up Southshore Drive toward Harry and Jane's. Out of the thickness of a moonless night the ghost-like figure of Canoe came into view. He walked right up to me. I picked him up and took him home.

But he had inadvertently cut short his required wild time. Taking him home was not where he wanted to be. His body was in the house, but his spirit was outside in the woods where moths flutter and owls hunt. I dropped him near Eva who was still clipping and sculpting her claws. I locked the doors, including the kitty door in the garage, and went to bed.

Canoe did not hang around Eva that night but retreated immediately to the garage, which Eva took as a personal snub. She found him, alone, under the car. She went back upstairs and continued her nails. Following the last application of polish, Eva went looking for him again. She searched the downstairs, including the garage, looked under the vehicles, and in all the corners, but Canoe was nowhere to be found. She looked in the downstairs guestrooms, the closet under the stairs, the bathroom cabinets. Even the tub. She went upstairs and looked everywhere. She went through our closet while I slept, moving clothes and shoes and long hanging robes until I wasn't sleeping any longer. Thank you. She opened every kitchen cabinet, thinking he may have closed it behind him. She looked under sofa pillows, in the piano, under the office desk. She went back downstairs and through the guestrooms, again. No Canoe.

She re-entered the garage and there he was.

Obviously he was in *Neverland*, the place where cats go when they don't want to be found. He, of course, acted nonchalant. "You looking for me?"

"Yes, I was looking for you. Where have you been?"

"Around."

"Around where?"

"You wouldn't understand. Besides, I don't know that I want to tell you."

This phenomenon of disappearance, reappearance has happened too often to be explained. It could be right up there with heaven, hell and UFO's.

Who knows where cats go or what they do "there." Maybe there's a bunch of cats in a crowded room playing pool and eating pizza. Maybe it's a southern church revival and they're under the big top, rocking to gospel music with their hands raised high.

Canoe ate with me in the morning while Eva slept, then disappeared outside to continue his roaming. Later that morning Eva got up and looked for Canoe, complaining that Canoe was very unapproachable last night. "He doesn't seem to be close to us anymore."

I've heard her say that before. She wants a clinging cat with fear of outside cats; not this distant cat that acts like a teenage kid eager to leave home and escape the grasp of his parents.

She recounted his reappearance from *Cat Neverland*, and said that she had searched the house from stem to stern only to find Canoe in the first place she had looked. She was sure he could not have hid from her, and I believe her. She went on about how she thought we are losing him, how he doesn't like us. "He comes home for meals, then leaves," she lamented. Having raised seven kids between us, we knew about this.

This is a mother who can find any kid's button, any mislaid keys, anything obscure, small, camouflaged and minuscule. I wouldn't call her small-minded, but she has the eyes of an eagle and the sleuth of a CIA agent. Daughter Amy will testify that if she even thought of doing anything wrong as a teenager, going anywhere where she was forbidden to go, thinking lecherously of any guy who was on mother's *I don't want you to see him anymore* list, the Mother would know it. This woman has antennae miles long and a head that scans like a satellite dish; she is clairvoyant, inquisitive, tirelessly perceptive and naturally suspicious. Canoe could not have evaded her.

Around lunch time Canoe came in, his coat ruffled and bearing a hundred seeds. Eva was putting lunch dishes away and he walked up to her and wrapped himself around her legs. All of her scolding and fretting and hours of deriding him for his indifference, his aloofness and his teenage withdrawal melted in a moment. He was back. He loved her. She looked down at him and smiled with tearing eyes and swooned, "My Canoeser is back."

Women are fickle. So are cats.

Chapter 34

Canoe Goes Camping

We were 75 miles down the road on an extensive trip to Minnesota and a family reunion in Colorado before we noted something dangling from our fifth-wheel trailer. We decided to take care of the problem and stop for lunch. We put Canoe in his new electric blue nylon harness in case he bolted from our arms as we carried him from the truck to the trailer. The trailer he knew. This was his home for four months and it was here that he met us.

He also knew where to hide, like behind the sofa where he could continue his travels to *Neverland*, the dimly lit foreign lands where badminton rackets were stored and awning poles lay like stacked wood. When we were living at the Crosseyed Cricket, he'd be gone for hours and we'd search the countryside for him; now here we were at a rest stop and in a flash Canoe had disappeared.

The basement cubbies of the trailer were a kind of low-light therapeutic center for Canoe. He'd zone out and find nirvana, maybe a cat library or sitting room where there were dark shades and an easy chair with a big hassock and good books, and the evening paper next to an end table with a snifter of brandy.

Eva would go berserk when Canoe escaped to these places, because a mother who doesn't see her baby is sure that something ill will befall it. A teenage boy, which is what Canoe was, had to give a full accounting of his presence and his activities lest he was cleaning his navel, picking his nose or doing something unseemly. The poor cat had no right to privacy as long as The Mother of Righteous Indignation was around.

Only with the removal of everything around the sofa and the contents of the basement cabinets did we find two golden eyes and that darling face looking at us. 'Trouble was, how do you get a hold of a cat who can dig in with twenty four hooks and make himself as permanent as an anchor snagged on a dead limb on the bottom of a creek.

I could get a finger through his harness, but that wasn't enough to pull him out. We were afraid his harness would get snagged on things and we'd have to dismantle the trailer or the cat to get him out.

Eva used his little fishing pole, dangling the "fish" (dead rabbit fur) in front of him, and she was almost successful. Canoe left his reclusive attitude for a moment to play, then figured things out and said, "No thanks. After a couple hours in that rattley truck with the roaring engine and the little rear seat made for midgets, I'd prefer to stay here. Thanks anyway."

Cute lasts just so long. Now it was a contest of wills, and Canoe was going to lose. That's what I thought, and I was the falcon. I was determined to get this darned cat out of his lair and back into the truck, so help me, God.

Eva and I began opening basement compartments on both sides of the trailer until we had a clean look at him, then with probes and prods we moved him in the direction of *THE FAL-CON* who grabbed him and never let go. If he had his hooks in rugs or badminton rackets, rugs or propane bottles, I would have torn them out.

Canoe, knowing a mad man when he sees one, submitted and let himself be picked up and marched over to the noisy pickup truck where he resigned himself to more boring hours in a back seat made for amputees.

Eva concluded, like mothers do when they're using feminine intuition and psychoanalysis, that when Canoe is fearful or when he encounters strange and threatening situations, he goes into himself and hides. He doesn't lean on his human companions for solace or protection. Son Alan may have run up and said, "Mommy, Mommy..." but not the cat.

Late in the afternoon of the first day of travel near the city of Richmond, Kentucky, the highway traffic ground to a halt at a highway construction site. Temperatures were in the nineties and everything was heating up. The truck engine began to overheat, which required us to shut off the air conditioning, which brought a rise in the temperature of the cat, the Mother and the driver. Northbound traffic was one long car lot with the pavement blistering and diesel engines from big trucks radiating heat like charcoal grills.

Canoe was distressed. His little pink tongue hung from his mouth with his sides panting. The Mother fussed over him, fearing he could get overheated and dehydrated. He wouldn't drink, so she took his medicine dropper and laid him back in her arms, placed the dropper in the corner of his mouth while depressing the bulb. He gulped and licked and in short order had a quantity of fluid in his belly. She placed a wet towel on the platform between the two bucket seats to cool him. For the time being Canoe had it better than we who sweated and stewed because the traffic was not moving and the banter over the CB indicated things would not improve quickly. It was about two hours before the line began to move again.

Later in the day we pulled into a campground and hooked up to electricity so we could run the air conditioning in the trailer. Life returned to normal and the hot blistering day was behind us.

Canoe settled into the ride after the first day of high temperatures and loud highway noises. At first, he roamed the truck, whining and appearing restless, but on the second day he seemed resigned and spent most of his time facing the air conditioning vents on the dash, or riding backward with the cool air moving over his body. A cat in a heavy fur coat on a ninety-degree day is in a difficult place.

We made it to Minnesota without further incidents. When Alan joined us in Minneapolis, Canoe had company and less space for himself. In the morning when the air was cool, we'd drive with the sliding window open to the bed of the truck. This would allow cool air to enter the cab and exit the vents on the front windows. Canoe took this as an invitation to do some "moon" walking, exiting the cab of the truck through the

open sliding window and walking on the tool chest that lay behind the cab. The strong wind whipped his long coat until he looked unkempt, but he was happy out there on his "sill" with passing vehicles and grazing cows and a constant changing panorama of things and obstacles. One slip on the slick painted surface, however, and he'd be road pizza, so Alan hung onto his leash...until the Mother saw what was going on and ordered Canoe back into the cab.

Mothers are no fun.

Near Mount Rushmore, Eva stepped outside the truck to photograph the carved figures of the presidents through a tunnel. Canoe was tied with his harness and leash to a handle on the side of the front seat, but seeing Alan and Eva alongside the road made him covet a walk in the woods, so he stood by the open window, then leapt for freedom, not realizing his restraints. His projection into space was short lived as he reached the end of his leash and swung abruptly against the truck door where he hung like fresh meat for a Rottweiler.

A passerby saw him dangling and said to him, "What are you doing hanging from your harness, pussy cat?" She picked him up and put him back in the truck again.

We're never sure that Canoe will return to us if he gets out despite his morning licks and kisses and his obvious (at times) devotion to us. When he wants to run, he treats us as the enemy. Probably only after he's tired and hungry would he come back to us again, if he could find us. With his charming personality and good looks, however, he could find a home anywhere.

Some of the time Canoe seemed to be tied to an imaginary tether, particularly when a dog was in the neighborhood; then getting him to leave the trailer was impossible. The door stood open and Canoe simply looked out. On other occasions he'd venture out, then scamper back in. The trailer had obviously become his home and asylum. But come night, when ghosts and goblins run through the woods, Canoe became emboldened and saw less danger.

Sometimes Canoe travels like a dog with his head out the window, the wind pulling back his hair and his big wet eyes drying in the 60 mph wind. At other times he sits on the console between the two bucket seats with fresh air coming in through the side vents.

Near Idaho Springs, Colorado, we stopped for gas and water and Eva and I shared a glass of ice water placed in the cup holders of the console between the seats, and in front of Canoe. He took this to mean that he was entitled also, so he sipped and we sipped, the three of us sharing one glass.

We were family. Don't talk to us about sanitation. Knowing where that little pink tongue has been requires blindness or family tolerance.

Chapter 35

Peter Rabbit Moves From the Garden to the Living Room

Domesticated hunting animals like cats must be torn between the impulse to bite and kill on one hand, and to bite and play on the other. For animals that get their food out of a bag or out of a can, they've got to be confused.

When Canoe goes out to hunt, he seems to be more intent on playing than killing and eating. There are raw animal impulses to hunt, to be sure, but Canoe is more like a photographer who bags his quarry with a camera. Tell this to a helpless mole in the grasp of a mouth of razor-sharp teeth.

The living things in his world can't tell cat "play" from "kill." And neither can Canoe. The more the squiggling mole or mouse or skink exerts to get away, the greater the pressure to keep it captive. The result is usually death, a playful death. It would be humane if Canoe would just get it over with and sink his spiky teeth into their skulls, but Canoe goes through the ritual.

One day Canoe was standing by the sofa, looking under it, then moving quickly to the rear of the sofa, then back to the front. He was in his hunting mode and he was excited. Something was under the sofa. I called to Eva and we watched him work. "I'll lift up the sofa and you catch the varmint."

"No!" she said, "I don't want to catch whatever is under there."

"Okay, YOU lift up the sofa and I'll catch the critter."

"No, go ahead. But I'm not promising to catch it."

I lifted the sofa and a bunny the size of a squirrel jumped out and tore around the room with Canoe in hot pursuit. Eva jumped, squealed and ran after him, hollering, "Get him, Ron. Get him!"

So, I'm after Peter Rabbit, Eva's after Canoe, the rabbit is after freedom and the neighbors across the woods are standing dead in their tracks listening to the mayhem coming from Timberlake Drive and wondering if they should call the sheriff.

Eva caught up with Canoe, I lunged for the bunny, the bunny squealed and I stood vis-à-vis with a terrified creature that felt little consolation in being in the hands of a 180-pound gorilla. I examined him and concluded that he was unharmed.

I took Peter to the edge of the forest and released him. He bounded away to his warren where he told the other bunnies the scary tale of a black and white cat that took him home to dinner. "But I got away from that ol' rascal cat, and I'm never going there again."

In the meantime back in the house, Canoe looked puzzled and seemed to say, "I only wanted to play with him, Dad."

The remarkable thing was that all the doors in the house were closed, so Canoe had to exit and re-enter by way of his cat doors. Obviously he had caught the rabbit in the woods, carried it into the house through the two cat doors, then up the stairs and into the living room where he played with his woodland friend, who was fit as a fiddle and remained that way until we caught him and released him.

Cats play hard. Little blue skinks try their hardest to escape, and this really turns Canoe on. If it isn't the claws that get them, it's the teeth. The skink, or any other creature, gets worn down from this game of catch and release and eventually collapses from trauma, cat breath, cat teeth or internal injuries.

When Canoe came in the house with a butterfly in his mouth one day, I scolded him. "C'mon, Canoe, for cryin' out loud. Butterflies are nice. Leave 'em alone. We want to see them in the garden, not in your mouth. Let loose of him."

For a moment Canoe seemed to listen to me. He opened his mouth and the butterfly flitted away. It was one of those magical moments when a cat opens his mouth and a butterfly emerges. But then he went mad with delight again as the butterfly streaked away. He and the butterfly were up the wall, onto the sills, around the lights. Finally I rescued the terrorized Lepidopteran and brought him outside where he had the advantage of height and trees. He just better not come down and smell our roses again.

Cicadas in the mouth and paws of Canoe end up with their wings bent or severed, circling and buzzing around on the outside deck like helicopters with damaged rotors. Canoe doesn't mind. A buzzing, flightless cicada is as good as a flying one…as long as they keep trying.

It makes you wonder why we have these kinds of animals as pets. Why do we love killers with no conscience, animals that seldom or never exhibit benevolence, generosity or kindness? Are we so taken by their beauty as they lie indolently on a sill on a quiet morning, or sit on our bookshelves as we go about our work? Are we pussy whipped by their purring? Weakened by their solicitous humility as they wrap themselves around our legs in the morning as we prepare breakfast? Are we fascinated with the mystery of their eyes, the seductive movement of their walk, their elusive personas and their coats of silken fur? Are we envious of their sanguine repose and their sleepy-eyed contentedness?

When are we going to rise up and say, "We're suckers, and we're not going to put up with this anymore?"

Chapter 36

Things Women Say to Cats

Eva: "You're so cute."

Canoe: "Whaddaya talkin' about?"

Eva: "You've got the cutest little butt. Your fur flares out like pantalettes. Canoe. I think you've got bloomers on."

Canoe: "Quit talkin' about my butt. What are you, some kind of pervert?"

E: "And that soft belly. I love to feel your soft belly."

C: "Take your hands off my private parts or I bite ya, lady."

"You're just like a bowl of jello. That little round belly. Look at that round belly..."

"You're disgusting. Do I come up to you and play with your belly and tell you it's like jello? Leave me alone."

"Look, Ron, he just rolls over and spreads his legs. You just love this, don't you, Canoe?"

"Okay, so I'm a sucker for fondling. Scratch me under the chin?"

"He's so confident we won't hurt him, he lies upside down. It's kind of sexy, don't you think, Ron?"

"For cryin' out loud, lady, I'm just cooling my crotch. You

see all that hair? I'm hot."

"Canoe, you are such a pretty boy. Ron, get my camera."

"Oh, jeez, now she's going to take my picture while I'm spread out here, I'll wait until she gets me all framed, then I'll roll over."

"C'mon, Canoe, get back over on your back and look relaxed. C'mon. Ron, will you help me turn Canoe over? He's not cooperating with me."

"Now I've got the big guy coming over. I'll have fun with him."

The Big Guy says gruffly, "Okay, Canoe. It's a Kodak moment. Let me take you over here in the sun and tickle your tummy."

"That's enough. Got birds to hunt and skinks to eat. Bye."

"Did you get the picture, Eva?"

"No, he wouldn't lay still and I wasn't ready."

Canoe went outside to watch the birds. When nobody was looking, he rolled over on his back again with his legs apart, looking up at the birds in the tree. It wasn't until the Big Guy rolled the screen door back and stepped outside with camera in hand that he rolled over on his belly and looked up with a cynical look.

"Yeah, Big Dude, whaddaya want?"

"Just a cheesy picture of you on your back, Canoe."

"What do you take me for? Some kind of a creature that lives for adoration and attention?"

"Hey, you're a cat."

"You got me there."

Chapter 37

Tag, You're "It"

I was watching a father with his daughter at a church function recently, and the daughter was playing with her friends. Occasionally, she'd come back to her father, touch him like a cat touches a human, a sliding, leaning movement that brought the two of them together for a moment, then she was gone again. It seemed that this reassuring touch was all she needed to explore the world beyond.

Canoe plays this game. He isn't happy being by himself, and after he's been out for a while, he comes to us for company. He'll come in and announce his return with an audible, "Hi, I'm home." It's only a squeak, but we know he's signaling his return. He'll sidle over, rub against us, often with a body brush, or nudge us with his head, and we'll reach out to him and talk to him and renew the contract. Then he'll walk away, catch a quick snack if there's anything in his food dish, then be gone again often to a peaceful corner to snooze.

Extended cuddling and holding isn't necessary or even desirable to him oftentimes. If we smother him with affection, he writhes himself free and seeks a private refuge. It's like playing tag; a touch is all the game requires, thank you.

The lingering look or the need to be close seems to be enough for both humans and cats. When Eva's at the computer in the office, Canoe will be outside the room looking in – looking at her… for minutes at a time, a drooling, "I adore you" look. And when Canoe takes his bulk and parks it on the desk in front of her, she thinks he's saying, "I love you and I want to be close to you." She'll reach out to him, bury her face in his; they'll both purr, then she'll go back to work and Canoe will continue his loving vigil. They're alike.

Canoe relaxs in the "in" box, or is that the "out" box on the desk of the office?

Chapter 38

Dr. Jekyll and Mr. Hyde

About five o' clock in the afternoon a year after he adopted us, our usually domestic, sleepy-eyed cat continued his transformation into a wild animal. It's not obvious; there is no coat color change, no strange look in his eyes, just a restless urging to be somewhere other than in the house. His citizenship shifts from Felis domesticus on Timberlake Drive to Felis beasticus.

He slips out of the house as surreptitiously as a thief and enters the uncertainty of blowing leaves, flitting shadows and the chill of evening that sends most domestic animals inside to a den with a fireplace.

It's disappointing to see him leave us every night. This is the time for the Homo sapiens to pour a glass of wine, light the fire and set aside the day's work. It's a peaceful time for humans. The shoes come off, the doors get locked and the house gets filled with the aroma of garlic and roasted meat.

And the cat goes out the door. "Hey, where you going, pussy cat?" we call. He doesn't flinch, doesn't flick his tail, gives no account of our solicitation.

He's flipped off the old cat and put on the new – the cat who keeps company with owls and animals with golden eyes that stare at each other and the moon.

Canoe has a kind of timer that runs down, then he's ready to come home. This timer runs out around 11 o'clock, then gets wound through the night and he's ready to begin the morning prowl around 5:00 a.m. He might go back to sleep again, or he might start hitting the roll of toilet paper in the bathroom. One of us will jump up, scold him, put him outside our bedroom and neglect him until we're ready to get up. He'll stay by the door, lying on the rug, waiting for us. Whether he sleeps that extended time, we have no idea. But there are times when we didn't heed his early morning alarm clock and he went back to sleep again.

By the time cat breakfast was over – a tablespoon of wet food, a half a dish of dried food – he was ready for a potty break, and there was no better place to do that than in the woods. Sometimes the need was so obvious, he would stop in the woods without scratching the ground and park his derriere unceremoniously and dump. I'd look and wonder if that was a real pit stop or was he just watching the wildlife. A turn and a gentle covering with dirt signified he had indeed just fertilized the forest. Then it was time to come back in and sleep. This was our awake time, time for early morning radio, a tennis game at 10, packages to the post office, stories to write, correspondence to take care. Canoe was asleep…underneath our feet, or in a corner by the piano. Canoe slept, waiting for the bewitching hour when domestic cats become feral again.

We get to have our cat for only half his life. The other half belongs to the wild side.

Chapter 39

"I Trust; Therefore, You (Must) Love"

That's pretty simplistic, I know, and it doesn't always work in human relationships. A trusting wife may find she has a wayward husband. And it doesn't work with all pet owners either. When Canoe lies on his back on the floor in the middle of the kitchen with his legs splayed out while we prepare a meal, we understand that here's an animal who is lying across the railroad tracks and is sure that we'll pull him off when the train comes.

He's watching from down there, and we're walking around and carrying dishes and a gallon of milk and a hot dish, and he's cool. A misstep or a dropped plate on his soft spots and he'd be off to the hospital. But he doesn't flinch, not even when I place my foot on his belly. Maybe it's the language I'm speaking and the way I do it. "Hey, Canoeser, what are you doing lying there in the middle of traffic? Don't you know we're cooking and we could step right on you and we could squish your little jelly belly? Look at that little belly. We're not going to feed you anymore until you slim down and begin doing some work around here, 'you hear? What do you think you are, the prince of the palace?

Well, let me tell you, fella, I'm gonna crack the whip and you're going to shape up. Now jump up and grab a towel. We've got some dishes to do."

The look in his eyes and position of his ears say he knows I'm kidding. He's safe. In fact, the more trusting he is with us, the more obligation we feel to earn the trust. Throwing himself open to our mercies somehow brings out the best in us.

Pussy whipping us in the morning is bald-faced manipulation, but it's so cute. There is no hanging on our legs with claws ripping the skin and screaming, "Feed Me, Feed Me." Rather, it's the kitty technique, a longing look, a sidewise slanting of the body against the leg which is a kind of full-body kiss. This is hard to resist, and even if he's now 15 pounds and he's as big as he should be, we find the impulse to give him more, because we love him, and we want him to love us. The more food we give him, the more he'll love us. Right?

We know this is nonsense. We usually catch ourselves in this trap before we reach for another spoonful. We don't want to make him a Cardiac Cat. Research indicates that animals like him, and us, age slower and are healthier if we're slightly underweight, so we exercise discipline and hope he understands.

He does. We reduce the size of his portions, and he doesn't wine like a kid, "Aw, c'mon Dad, I need more than that. I've got squirrels to chase and a driveway to guard, and if it wasn't for me those tufted titmice and black capped chickadees would eat us out of house and home. How about another tablespoon full? Pleeeze."

Likewise with him lying on the bed. I don't like 15 pounds of tiger between my legs when I'm sleeping, and I want him off, but he wants to be near us and I like that. But how do I push away my lover without spurning his love? I send him to Eva lying next to me, who has shorter legs. Canoe can find more room at her end of the bed, and besides, she's more tolerant...more loving.

But then comes 7:30 a.m. and sunrise. Canoe is ready for another day of titmice watching and driveway guarding, and he'll come up and lie on my chest and nuzzle me. I look like sin. He doesn't care.

What do I do? Launch him onto the floor? He just kissed me. My mental state is a blend of ghoulish paranormal and faulty morning reality. But I have enough judgment to know a kiss when I get one. I'm happy anybody loves me in the morning.

Canoe stretches out in a beautiful crescent shape
in a cunning effort to get more food.

Chapter 40

Move over, Canoe

We weren't aware how much Canoe had grown in the year and a half since he came to live with us. When son Jeff came in February, he looked at Canoe and said, "What have you been feeding him?" Jeff saw Canoe seven months earlier in the summer when Canoe was not wearing his Norwegian fur coat, but in the winter Canoe sports a lion's mane of hair that is so rich and full it often gets in his mouth.

We've decided that he is closest to a Norwegian Forest Cat, a thick bodied, heavy-coated cat with big paws and the mane of a lion, but of course, Canoe's heritage is east of the tracks and south of the speedway, and somewhere between the shack in the woods and the cement block factory.

One day I saw a delicate little orange cat walking along the sidewalk of our Tennessee home. The little cat was walking feebly, favoring her right, rear leg so that she had a peg leg gait. Eva and I were both at computers, but my station faces outward, a view I relish, and any bird on the wing or legged creature of the wood catches my eye.

When I told Eva there was a cat sauntering down our side-

walk, she immediately left her work and went to the front door
to investigate. We have had a number of intruders, and most of
them have been unfriendly and a threat to Canoe who, despite
his bulk and lion's mane, is a pussycat of the first order and
avoids confrontations.

Eva caught up with the little strawberry blonde at the end
of the front walk. She was moving slowly and without determination. She didn't seem to have any destination in mind, just
walking. When Eva called to her, she stopped and meowed. Eva
approached her and extended a hand. The little cat came up to
her, mildly meowing until they were eye to eye. Cats respond to
the soft touch of a cat-lover's hand. I think it's Eva's small stat-
ure, tender approach and the allowance for the cat to respond.
The little cat responded as most cats do; she came right up to
Eva, so Eva picked her up and caressed her. She was almost past
kittenhood, but she was a mere handful of blonde fur and bones.

"Where have you been, little kitty, and where are you going?" Eva asked.

She came back to the house with the cat and we looked the
little kitty over, determined her sex and tried to piece together
her state of affairs. Was she abandoned? Did she belong to someone in the neighborhood? In her present state of starvation and
dehydration, it wasn't likely she had a real home. Her back leg
looked like it had been broken, but was healing, although not
quite straight.

Eva and I talked about what to do with her, and I heard
Eva say clearly, "We don't want another cat. We'll have to find a
home for her."

I agreed, and inasmuch as we were going to the county
seat later in the day where Animal Welfare was located, we'd

take the kitten along and see to her care at the animal shelter.

We put out food and she ate like a lion. We gave her milk, which she consumed like a hot horse after a rough ride. She devoured the remainder of Canoe's wet food, then went to his dry food dish, which she licked clean. I thought she would burst.

"Eva, I think we ought to give her a rest," I said, "she can't possibly assimilate anymore food, although I'll bet she would eat it if we put it out for her."

I got on the phone to the Loudon County Animal Welfare, but it was President's Day. The phone rang, no one answered. Finally a taped message came on stating they were closed Sundays and holidays. Our run to the animal shelter to get rid of the cat was foiled. Secretly, Eva was delighted. Secretly, I was too. Neither of us wanted another cat, but neither of us was ready to give the loveable, needy blonde away.

She was long in the trunk and full in coat, although she had the look of an old fur coat that had grown ragged with age. She was probably about six months old, weighed about four pounds and still had her baby teeth.

Canoe was very interested in the little lady, and wanted to

play, so we put her in the downstairs bathroom where Canoe would not disturb her while we did some errands. This would give her time to digest some of that big breakfast. She was adjusting to a new environment, a full belly and the fatigue that accompanies homeless life in the winter.

How does anyone with compassion for living things, turn down an animal who meekly asks for help? Blessed even more are those who comfort and feed ugly animals that bite.

Independently both Eva and I were thinking about names for her, although neither of us was committing to adoption. The circumstances were similar to the way that Canoe came to us. In the car on the way home from our errands, we approached the subject of names for the cat. We knew that this is tantamount to adoption, but we went ahead with the game anyway. Eva suggested, Miss Volly, because the school color of the Volunteers of the University of Tennessee is orange. I countered with Imogene, Eva's middle name. She nixed that. I suggested Lelia, Eva's sister who also had orange-blonde hair. "I'm not going to name a cat after my sister," she scowled.

"How about Reba? Reba McEntire is a strawberry blonde," I said.

"Yeah, that's good," Eva said.

A cat's name should be two syllables so when you're calling them it can be said easily, "C'mere, Reba."

Following our errands, we looked in on Miss Reba. She jumped off her "bed" and greeted us. We took her back upstairs and fed her again.

The day before Reba came to live with us, Canoe came in with a purple finch. The poor bird was still breathing and struggling and I scolded Canoe for his (lack of) wilderness ethic. I held the traumatized bird in my hand and tried to comfort it in its last few minutes of life. I hate this about cats. Our feeder is off the back deck and I spill generous quantities of seed on the railing so we have a congregation of birds outside our window. Canoe spends endless hours watching, and obviously couldn't resist the temptation to catch one. The mouth of a cat on the fragile airframe of a bird is sure to destroy their aeronautical skills, not to mention the psychological trauma of being in a mouth full of fangs. The little bird came to life in my hand, opened its eyes again and attempted to escape, but the landing gear and the wing assembly had been seriously damaged.

What does one do with one of God's little ones that is dying? Repent for the sins of your cat, which you brought into this house? I placed the finch in a box with lots of packing for insulation, and waited. The end, mercifully, came within an hour.

Now we had another potential killer on our hands. Reba, true to her heritage, would be a bird killer too. Wildlife does not thrive near the hunter's den.

Through that first day, the question of whether to have another cat in the house occupied most of our thinking. Reba lounged in the study near us where we worked. Part of the time she spent on Eva's lap, partly on mine. Then she lay at our feet as we moved about and wrote. What would we do with her through the night? With her wounded leg, could she get in and out of the litter box?

Later in the day we had another reality event that colored our decision. Canoe caught another bird. The feeder off the back deck has become his favorite place to watch and hunt. Why not? I've induced birds into our immediate environment and Canoe is one of the beneficiaries. It's a two-fold feeder — one for the birds, the other for the cats.

I was at the computer when I heard Canoe in the living room. There was tremendous sound and motion, and the rug was filled with black litter, which I didn't immediately recognize as feathers; but Canoe had caught up with his quarry again. I shamed him, took the little Junco that was still alive and tried to comfort it. I was very apologetic.

I put the wounded bird in our bathroom wash basin lined with a towel, and shut the door. Maybe the poor little thing would recuperate. Maybe it would die. I couldn't stand there and watch.

An hour later I walked into the washroom/recovery room to see how the little bird was doing. It looked up at me with shiny black eyes and moved slightly. I went to pick it up, but it flew out of the basin and into the mirror. It could fly. I picked it up, went outside and opened my hand. The little guy flew through the woods, swooping down to a pile of brush. With no tail feathers, it did very well, and I hoped that the spring molt and summer plumage would bring it new life.

By the time we were ready for bed, we had decided nothing, except that we liked this little cat. She was gracious and showed her thankfulness by rubs and touches. But Canoe, she thought, was a useless, annoying and unnecessary part of the hospice. If we hoped that Canoe would gain some feline companionship, it was not developing with Reba.

We decided to put her in the downstairs bathroom overnight with the pet carrier, which we had warmed and lined with a big, soft towel. Food and water were nearby as well as Canoe's original little litter box. We closed the door and promised we'd see her in the morning.

Lord help us. What should we do with this cat?

Chapter 41

Please, Don't Leave Me

We heard Canoe bleating in the morning. His meows were little squeaks and he wasn't upstairs. We jumped out of bed and followed the sound. Canoe was at the downstairs bathroom door wondering about Reba who doubtless was stirring and probably meowing. She was wondering if the Good Samaritans were going to get up and feed her again.

Eva and I were in our pajamas, standing barefooted in the bathroom watching Reba while Canoe made a quick examination of her, then went into the carrier where she had spent the night. He wanted to play with her, swiping her as she passed him in the bed-in-a-crate, but she was not to be played with. She wanted affection, and she wanted food.

Reba had been in the house for nearly 24 hours now. Her gimpy leg still had a swelling at the first joint, but touching her leg did not evoke the same squeals, and she walked on all fours mostly, at times stretching out the bum leg. Maybe the antibiotic was helping. We'd given her a dropper full of Canoe's antibiotic a couple of times the first day. After we carried her upstairs we gave her another dose, then set her down next to the food dishes by the refrigerator.

Eva talked about taking her to the vet, but I said we have to agree to adoption before we invest much money in her. Not that I didn't want to do what's right, and it's really not the vet bill; it's going all the way in our commitment before we had rationally thought of the consequences of another cat in the house…and in the travel trailer… and in the boat. Managing ourselves seems to be a task oftentimes, now we'd have two kids to think about, too.

If we went to the vet and she was cured and got healthy, did that mean she stayed with us? If she continued to limp and her leg swelled, did that mean she was too sick to stay with us and we'd take her to the animal shelter and let them deal with it? Maybe they had a visiting vet who took care of remedial ailments in the shelter's population.

I could argue that she was just another hillbilly cat with no pedigree…or culture…or special features. I could do that with the purple finch that Canoe caught a night ago also. I could do that for Canoe. I could do that for each of us. Yet, each of us has the magic of the divine. A cat, for cryin' out loud, uses a litter box without reading the instructions.

Reba, like Canoe, had excellent deportment. No soiling of rugs or upholstery, no boisterous behavior, no obnoxious demands — just a grateful look, a meek submission to reality and the wishful look in her eyes that we wouldn't make her experience any more hardship and starvation that brought her to our doorstep.

Reba drank warm milk until I thought she'd burst, ate all the wet food put out for her, then attacked a bowl of dry food. At the same time, Canoe was given his share on the other side of the kitchen, but soon Reba went over to him and nudged him out of place. Canoe swiped at her; she cowered. He stood by wondering what to do next; she resumed eating his food while he stood by and watched. Four pounds of female determination displaced fifteen pounds of male uncertainty. Pussy whipped never had a more poignant demonstration.

We knew Canoe was a wimp, but this was a little surprising given other interactions where Canoe initiated play with Reba and she avoided any encounter.

Reba didn't seem to know how to play. Neither gray mouse on a fishing line nor Canoe's favorite pink plastic egg was any attraction. Her only interest seemed to be cuddling and kneading. Her front feet were in constant motion, like a kitten working it's mother's teats. She seemed to be in an extended infantile state, needing to be fondled and fed.

Eva said to Reba in a mild rebuke, "If you can't be good company for Canoe, you can't live here." Reba looked sad with her little kitty face and didn't understand.

I called the county animal shelter to see what their procedure would be with Reba. Do they have a visiting vet? Are they equipped with antibiotics? What would they do with her if they couldn't fix her leg? The person answering the phone assured me that Ramona, the primary caregiver, was able to work magic on sick pets and had a pretty good medicine cabinet to take care of wounds and lesions.

We decided that Reba needed to see someone with more knowledge than we had, and if they could fix her up, either we would come back for her or we'd wait to see if another family would adopt her. We had already tallied the cost of another animal, the inconvenience when we traveled, and most importantly, companionship for Canoe. We weren't sure that Reba would be his playmate, although one day was a little too early to tell. We didn't just want another cat in the house; we wanted somebody to run Canoe's fanny. Maybe he'd leave the birds alone if he had another feline attraction.

So we drove out to Loudon County Animal Welfare, past the recycling yards and into Ramona's smoke-filled cathouse. She was there and took Reba and placed her in a clean cage lined with newspapers. Around the perimeter were other displaced cats, some sleeping, some leaning against the rear wall in shame or depression, some rubbing into the grates pleading for adoption. A beautiful tuxedo cat had just come in. He'd used the sofa as a toilet that morning and the owner immediately trundled him off to animal welfare. "It's going to be hard to find a home for him," Ramona said, "but Reba is so sweet. We'll find a place for her."

Reba went into her cage and immediately leaned out. "Please don't leave me here."

We filled out the paper work and left.

"Well, how do you feel, you cold hearted woman?" I said to Eva as we drove away.

"I'm okay with this. They will probably be able to get her well again, and Ramona thinks she's imminently adoptable. I want a cat that will be company for Canoe." We left it at that.

We think we did the right thing. We thought that maybe in a day or two we'd have regrets, but sweet-faced Reba was not in our present, and we trusted she was going to make a darling lap kitty for someone who needed her as much as she needed someone to love her. I could see a recent widower…, a lonesome guy who just broke up and needed someone warm nearby… or a kid who was misunderstood and needed something to cuddle.

Chapter 42

Canoe Finds a Playmate

The next day we got a call from Ramona at county animal welfare. A woman and her daughter had just come in looking for a cat. Reba saw them coming and gave them her most needy, pleading look, leaning into the bars and begging for attention. For a little girl looking for a lap kitty, this was a Godsend.

They were informed of Reba's condition, but a day in Ramona's cathouse with heavy doses of antibiotics were restorative enough to put Reba on the road to recovery. By the time the lady and the young girl arrived, Reba was walking on all fours with little discomfort.

The paper work was filled out and the fees paid. Reba left the smoke filled cathouse for a house and a home with a little girl who held her tightly and promised with all the sincerity a little girl can muster, that she would love and adore her until death do us part.

We were relieved and happy with this set of circumstances. We rescued Reba at a critical stage, gave her the food and water she needed to turn the corner from starvation to self-sufficiency, and had the chance to put her in the hands of an angel. It was the first smoking angel we had encountered, but angels are not held to logical circumstances.

When we left on a Florida vacation, we had to find a place for Canoe to stay. Dr. Geoffrey Riggin had treated him when he had was attacked by Slobedon, and Janie, who ran the office, was fond of Canoe.

Veterinarians often have a resident cat and Lenny was the cat who had the run of the place. He greeted everybody who came through the door and should you sit for a time, he'd have the buttons right off your pockets. He was a small neutered male, mostly white with patches of tabby and orange on his face and his back, and was half the size of Canoe. The first encounter between Lenny the lightweight and Canoe the heavy weight was suspicion. There was typical cat hissing, but as time went on, they played together like two-year olds with lots of rough and tumble play.

The alliance with Lenny gave Canoe resident cat status, too. He had the run of the place and the chance to lie in wait in doorways of the rooms where he would waylay Lenny as he came around a corner. A lot of pawing, swiping and full body checks ensued in the days ahead, with Canoe invariably (graciously?) on the bottom with his big paws in Lenny's face. Lenny would bite the wool carpet that Canoe was still wearing as winter waned, and came up with mouths full of white down. He'd gag and writhe trying to get his mouth clear of Canoe's fir, and Canoe would look up from his lower birth at Lenny who was dealing with an oral problem.

We knew Canoe was in a safe and friendly environment, so we left him there for a week. We missed him and were eager to pick him up when we returned. When Eva came into the office, Janie called out, "Canoe, your mommy's here."

She opened the door to the back room and Canoe came out where Eva stood, her arms outstretched in smiling anticipation. Canoe looked, glanced at Lenny who was rounding a corner and ran and pounced on him, oblivious and callously indifferent to The Mother. Where did loyalty go? Where was the affection she so solicitously sought?

"Canoe, we've been gone and I missed you. Didn't you miss me?"

Eva watched their playful roughhousing for a few moments before she picked up Canoe, and forced him to acknowledge her. She paid the bill and drove home. As she came up the stairs with Canoe in her arms, she complained, "He wasn't even glad to see me, the brat. He had this other cat he was playing with and hardly had time to notice me."

She put Canoe down and it was like setting down a peck of potatoes. He just sat there. Was he confused about where he was? Was he missing the kennel and Lenny and the traffic of animals? Was he in love with Lenny and Janie? Janie admitted she got lots of licks from Canoe.

As the day progressed, Eva became convinced that Canoe was in a funk. He was home, but he was not at home. He wanted to go back to Dr. Riggin's place and play with Lenny.

"Ron, I think he needs a playmate."

"Honey, we've been through this before. We could have kept Reba."

"Yeah, but she wasn't any company to him. You should have seen him with Lenny. They played and played. This is what he needs."

The following day, Canoe showed no improvement. His attachment to us was growing but there was lethargy we had never seen before, a detached, longing look back that we interpreted as, "You brought me back from a place that was a lot more fun than this place. I'm going to pout and you're going to suffer."

In a flippant moment I said, "Maybe they have a cat like Lenny over there that needs a home. Why don't you give them a call."

It was like saying to a teenage girl that she could go on a date. In a nanosecond Eva was ringing the vet's office. "Hi, this is Eva Stob. We picked Canoe up yesterday..."

"Oh, Hi, Eva. We miss Canoe and Lenny does, too. When are you going to bring him back..."

"Well, probably soon. But meanwhile, do you know of any playful cats that would be good company for Canoe? We're thinking of getting him a playmate."

Chapter 43

Cruising with Canoe

It was a maiden voyage of sorts, both for the first mate, the captain, the cat and the 13 year-old cruiser we christened, *Li'l Looper*. We were dirty and exhausted from the preparations for cruising the Cumberland River, and in a moment we tried desperately to acquire the attitude of fresh explorers.

The Cumberland River helped. The quiet beauty of this meandering river and its towering rock formations calmed us and we slumped in repose to the salving peace of the river. God surrounded us with his garden, the birds sang and the world looked new.

There were cormorants running on the water as we rounded the river bends. Limestone cliffs with eroded caves, cedars growing on top with dogwood and redbud along the slopes make the upper Cumberland exceptionally beautiful.

But Canoe was down in the galley finding comfort in close surroundings, sometimes backing himself into corners or into cabinets. When the boat was running, Canoe was withdrawn. In fact, he was in a funk. He was happy only when the boat stopped and the day's lights went out.

We cruised upriver from Granville, Tennessee, to Celina, plying the navigable headwaters of the Cumberland River, then we turned around and found an anchorage for the night. This was a good time for Canoe. The engine was quiet; there were critters on the water and on the shoreline and he forgot he was on a moving platform. In fact, as evening deepened, Canoe became emboldened and stood on the back seat cushions, looking over the water, then stepped onto the side step that leads to the narrow walkway around the boat. Gingerly he stepped outside, turned and walked toward the bow.

In the minute that you turn away from a cat, it appears in another place. When we looked up and didn't see him anywhere inside, we looked to the bow and found him in a state of feline reverie, examining rising bubbles in the water and listening to the call of geese in the distance.

We were apprehensive watching Canoe walk across the slippery surface of a fiberglass boat, because claws don't work here and there is no safeguard for a cat save their sure footedness. The mother went out, talked to her baby and gently took him in her arms and worked her way back to the cockpit while I watched in somewhat anxious anticipation.

We rehearsed what we would do if he fell in. We'd bought a large fish net to scoop him up, but if he swam away from the boat in a state of panic, there was no doubt that I was the designated savior. I'd be in the water trying to save a cat with claws that would either see me as a raft or as a further threat. I didn't argue with Eva. Canoe needed to be inside.

At the marina Canoe walked the docks on a leash, winding himself and the 20 foot cord around anchors, stanchions and fishing poles until he was in total gridlock and we had to unwind him in the dark and bring him in. The problem could be that if he jumped from one boat to another, or across water from a dock to a boat, he'd reach the end of his tether and he'd end up dangling.

No matter how many times we have entered locks, it's still a kick to be in a great flushing tub with the swooshing of water as each of the baffles on the lock gate sucks water and we drop to the next level. Inside Cordell Hull Lock swallows swarmed and Black Crown Night Herons fished from the walls of the locks. This got Canoe's attention as the birds called and hunted from the rim of the descending lock.

We had a wonderful evening in our anchorage at Saunder's Branch. In the morning it was cool and drizzly. We were up at 7:30, but it was 10 o'clock before we were underway. It was raining so we busied ourselves doing chores, cleaning the anchor and searching for Canoe who might have gone overboard or was hiding in one of the numerous pouches and stowage compartments of the boat. We had to turn the boat inside out to find him. We continue debating the merits-demerits of having a cat aboard. Eva is attached to this animal, and so am I, but I'm sure Canoe would rather be at the Vet's office with his playmate Lenny than be on this moving platform with us. He doesn't complain, however; he just seems out of sorts, sullen, withdrawn, coping and existing. Takes after me.

Finally we arrived in the city of Nashville, not pretty from the water's edge. This was after all, a working man's town before it became a mecca for recording and performing artists. Canoe was settling in to the cruise by the time we got to Nashville. It was Sunday and we had been on the water since Tuesday. He sat on the edge of the boat as it rocked at the dock, or jumped off and walked the docks. We watched attentively because there was a nearby wooded slope that looked good to him and from his past performance we were sure that if he got on shore, he'd be gone exploring for who knows how long.

On one occasion when he was walking the docks, he stopped to look over the edge of the pier into the mirrored water of the Cumberland River and saw an image of a cat just like him. He jumped back in startled amazement, his ears pinned back, looking all about for a cat that might surface at any moment and attack him.

Then he walked down the dock a bit further and slowly looked over the edge again. There was that same cat with the big yellow eyes and the ears pinned back, obviously following him along the dock, but down below. He jumped back again with heightened fear in his eyes and body, his head spanning the deck around him. He couldn't believe it. He could not get rid of this Neptune feline that showed its head everytime he looked down.

Canoe repeated this scene time and again, each time jerking back and looking around suspiciously. Finally he walked a straight line back to me, his ears down, his rear end dragging like a low rider and unhesitatingly jumped on the boat and ran to the safety of the salon where I think I heard him say, "Man, that was spooky. There's some weird-lookin' cat down there in that water. And he looked just like me!"

The next night we anchored in the Harpeth River that had the milt of spring flora on the surface, giving the river a textured appearance. *Li'l Looper* cut her way through this post orgasmic melange, leaving a path, until we found a suitable place to drop the hook.

The woods were full of bird songs and sex was in the air. The wind had lost its energy and the air lay heavy and still. The buzzards were doing their last of the day soaring and wrens and vireos chattered from the bush. Great Horned Owls hooted their territorial calls and a barnyard dog barked from the distance. Canoe was enjoying this and was a picture of contentment, a state of affairs he enjoys only when the boat is stopped.

Eva was hankering for a catfish dinner, so we put Canoe in the galley/salon, closed the door and went overboard to the dinghy for a ride to the mouth of the Harpeth River to Dozier's Restaurant for catfish dinner. A sign at the door noted there was not a waitress on duty, so we ordered at the window, seated ourselves and cleaned our table before we left. Not a bad arrangement.

We got back to the boat, opened the door to the galley and let Canoe have a run of the boat while we read and prepared for bed. Around 10 o'clock we heard the rumbling of thunder in the distance and moved quickly to put up all the camper canvas on the boat. The mother checked on her baby before she came to bed and announced that he was nowhere to be found. We looked in cabinets, under the bed, went back up to the helm and looked in all the cubbies that stored fenders and line. Canoe was missing. The mother's temperature and anxiety was rising. We retraced our steps, re-examined the cupboards again. Maybe he got into the refrigerator. No Canoe. Could he be outside? The weather by this time was showing strength. I unsnapped the canvas on the starboard side and there was Canoe backing toward me from the bow. He looked distressed and uneasy and made a quick entrance inside when the canvas was loosened. He retreated to the salon and stood there catching his breath.

For several days following this event Canoe seemed again to be in a funk, and he moved as if he had muscle pain. We wondered if he had a near fall and had to cling to a stanchion when/if he lost his footing on the glossy fiberglass. From that point on in the trip he was more cautious, but cats are cats and if there is another moonlit night with fish jumpin' you can be sure his curiosity will get him near the edge and along the slippery walkway so he can have some quality time on the bow examining all of creation.

Canoe helps Ron at the helm of our boat, Li'l Looper.

Chapter 44

There's a Mouse in the House

I was awakened in the middle of the night by running in the house. Eva was running and Canoe was running and Eva was quietly squealing (as quietly as any woman squeals when they see a mouse). Canoe was on the hunt again.

Mice don't walk into our house. There are better things for a mouse to do in the woodpile and in the forest. Nuts abound and there's a ton of seeds to eat. It's Canoe. He invites them into the house. Not of their own free will, of course. They're usually coming in in his mouth, lying crosswise under his whiskers like a chef would lay a side of beef ready to cut for a buffet.

And after he's got it in the house it's time to take a serious look at it. Drop it from your mouth and hold it with one foot. But the hold with the gauzy paws and embedded blades is not sufficient intimidation for a mouse bent on survival. A mouse can eye a crack big enough for itself and too big for a cat, and can move quicker than Eva can squeal, "There he goes, get him, Canoe, get him!"

I, of course, was invited to the party at 1:27 a.m. A hunter I am not, and especially at 1:27 a.m. standing there in my nightshirt and baggy eyes wondering what would be a cool first move. I guess I'll go to the living room where the little woman is wide-eyed and bushy tailed following Canoe who is wide-eyed and bushy tailed. Canoe was darting across the rug after the elusive mouse, cutting like a quarter horse, weaving and dipping, shooting forward, his pupils dilated, his muscles quivering.

The mouse darted under the sofa, panting and giggling, "That fat ol' pussy cat can't get me under here. Nyah, nyah, nyah, nyah. I can almost tweak his whiskers. I'll taunt him until he digs a hole in the carpet or in the sofa. Then we'll see who's the bad guy. I can stay here all night. Goodnight, pussy cat."

But I had ideas for removing the uninvited guest. I know, it wasn't his fault that he was in the house and now under the sofa, but the mouse had to go. So I slowly lifted the sofa, and voila. No mouse. Maybe he went under the settee. I lifted it, and the disclosed mouse made a dash down the hall for the bedroom. Same bedroom where I wanted to go back to sleep. Canoe sniffed him out. Under the dresser. "Canoe, that dresser weighs a ton. My back is sore and I'm cold and I don't want to lift that thing."

"Sorry, dad, but that's where I think he went. You want to get back to bed or not?"

So I pulled out a top drawer and lifted with all my might, my soggy night muscles coming to hardness as the dresser came away from the wall. Canoe looked behind and beneath in the space big enough for a mouse. Eva got a flashlight and the two of them lay on the floor, their heads together, the beam of the flashlight sweeping to the corners of the dresser…nothing. Eva quickly picked up the comforter and the throw pillows that lay on the floor. The mouse could be hiding in there and jump out just when you lifted it. No mouse.

Maybe it was behind the bureau, heavy as a mothah. I pulled it from the wall. Nothing. Canoe looked perplexed. I looked tired. Eva looked relieved but perplexed. If the mouse was still in the room, where was he? And would we feel him in the middle of the night if he ran across the bed?

I went back to bed. All the bedroom furniture was pulled away from the walls, the living room furniture was askew and a mouse was on the lam somewhere beneath our feet.

I thought of how the mouse felt. He was small, defenseless, meant no harm, neither swore nor drank, lived a peaceful life in the woods with the deer and the opossum, didn't want to come into the house, preferred to be outside and absolutely hated to be hunted and played with. He only wanted his family and his Mommy and some nuts, and we were treating this harmless beady-eyed little creature as if he were a dragon. We were afraid it would run across our bodies or sit on our chests and stare us in the eye. I was 183 pounds, he was 4 ounces, maybe. What's wrong with this scene? I went to sleep, but glanced over at Eva who was wide-eyed and wondering when the monster would attack.

In the morning I was doing leg tucks before getting out of bed. Canoe came over from the nightstand and tucked his body beneath my fanny. I sent a hand down to say hello, and we held paws for awhile. I tried to feel the hidden sabers in his downy paws. He took this for romance and play, and tenderly nipped me.

"You're a pain in the patoot in the middle of the night, Canoe." He nibbled me again. I grasped his head in my hand and held it for a moment, then let go and he licked me. We had an agreement. I would never hurt him; he could trust me to be nice and to take care of him, and in case I had an inkling to strangle him, he would roll over and be cuddly and gently nibble my fingers and I'd melt into admiration and affection.

I'm so weak, so easily bought and manipulated. I was amazed at myself and my quick change of mood. I was also impressed with my love for this beast and I heard myself saying, "This can't be love, Canoe, you're only a cat."

Chapter 45

Killing is Boring

At least that's the impression you get when you see a cat "play" with a mouse. Canoe brings a mouse into the house and we'll find him in the kitchen, if we find him at all, with the mouse cornered and Canoe nearly asleep. "Ho hum, I got a mouse. Not a lot of fun really."

The wee mouse will size up the laissez faire attitude of the cat and BOLT, and the cat who we thought had sleeping sickness will become as mean as Mike Tyson and will turn into a flurry of slipping paws and gleaming eyes. He'll catch the mouse and WAP it back into his corner. Tumble…tumble…tumble. "Ooh, that hurts".

Then Canoe will get dreamy-eyed again while the little mouse tries to figure out how that dumb cat went from 0 to 120 in .00002 seconds. The mouse will make his move subtly, a little at a time, then GO FOR IT! Canoe flips on the after burners, catches up to the mouse - SMACK! Tumble…tumble…tumble, back to its corner.

The puny mouse in his confusion and hysteria may run into Canoe and Canoe will cuff him and hold him and the mouse will go for cover beneath Canoe's black and white fur. Hardly a place of refuge for a mouse, but Canoe thinks its cool, and he'll go to sleep, the lion and the lamb lying together. It's so cute. But if Canoe absent-mindedly gets up and finds a mouse in his coat, it's the GREAT ESCAPE routine with Canoe in hot panting pursuit swiping with saber claws.

The last episode that oscillates between war and sleep is anything but peaceful. Once he has made the kill, he doesn't quit. He'll play with the carcass as if he's trying to bring it back to life. He's so sorry he's killed it.

He'll give life to it if it has none of its own; moles and skinks can be dead for hours and he's still administering life support – toss it into the air, flip it over his body, fling it against the wall, anything to get it to move. What's deviant behavior to us is clean fun to a cat.

Eventually the mouse gets eaten. Canoe begins at the front and works his way back. First, eat the snout, then the eyes and then the brains. He won't eat the entire thing, just the tasty parts. Yes, we have a smart cat. 'Gets his brains from his mice. YUK! And this is the same cat that gives us licky kisses in bed.

"Go away!"

Chapter 46

Behaviors To Emulate

Why do we love cats? I ponder the question.

Cats have a number of things going for them, their handsome coats, their pretty faces, the long following tail and their cuddly feeling, The tactile sensations are no doubt part of our relationship with them, but we love them differently than we love a stuffed animal or a fur rug. If our family cat was a taxidermist's model, I don't think we'd pet it and rub our hands across its fur and carry on in baby talk. Well, maybe we would, but it would be a once-a-week thing and we would only do it when no one was looking.

There's something in the *nature* of a cat that we like. If these behaviors work for a cat, maybe they'd work for a spouse. There may be some examples for us guys that will enhance our relationship with our wives.

Cats are aloof. When you call their name it's like you're talking to a flowerpot. Oftentimes I have to raise my voice, "Canoe…Canoe…CANOE!" Only then will I get a glance or a look. And the look doesn't say, "I'm sorry, I was thinking about mice and skinks. Forgive me. Yes, you wanted to talk with me?"

Husbands are aloof and where does it get us? I don't see our stock going up.

Cats make lots of body contact. In bed he'll be right up against us. Invariably we'll cuddle him, scratch him behind the ears, run our hands from his neck to his fanny.

Guys try this. Do you think we get cuddled, scratched behind the ears, stroked from our necks to our fannies? Not a lot. Not enough.

Cats beg to be fed with licks on the cheeks, on the mouth, in the corner of the nose.

Try this guys. "What's wrong with you? Go take a shower. Take a walk."

Cats bring into the house things from the outer world – wingless swallowtail butterflies, tailless skinks, decapitated mice. Women invariably describe this behavior as "He's bringing us a love gift."

I bring in boat carburetors, broken water pumps, an opossum skull found in the garden. Do you think my woman swoons? "My hubby brought me a love gift." You can see the words forming, can't you? "Get out of here with that."

Cats approach their food dish, eat a little and go out to play.

You can get away with this when you're a kid, but when you have a wife you're expected to eat what's put in front of you and then help with the clean up. "And, oh honey, after you clean up, will you take the garbage out and fix the sink? And don't forget the lawn, and then help me put the new hydrangea in the ground."

Cats lie across the house like ornaments. They lounge on the piano, across the hearth, on the sofa, deck, front porch, sidewalk, bed stands.

Lying across the piano might well get a call from the county psychiatric field worker. And lying naked in front of the fireplace…? "What are you doing? Get up. What if Jehovah Witnesses come to the door!"

Cats come in, the caregiver picks them up and holds them against their breast. The cat responds with legs spread wide in total surrender.

I come in and I don't get nothin'. Maybe it's, "Honey, we've got some bad mail. The bank says we're…the stock market took a dump today…"

I'd love to hear her say, "Oh that's my cuddle bundle, Oh, you're so soft (or hard)." Yeah, sure.

Cats sleep 80% of their lives.

That shouldn't be too hard; but don't count on getting any points for this. You may get the prize for the dopiest, dullest husband in town.

Cats sleep around – in the garage, in the spare bedroom, in the dungeon, underneath the stairs.

I don't sleep around. Maybe it's worth a try.

Cats jump right into your lap when you're reading the paper and expect this to be interpreted as loving and thoughtful.

Go ahead. Try this.

Cats "go" outside and consider this perfectly normal.

If I should be outside working and nature calls and I'm seen facing a tree with my hands in front of me I'm considered a savage. Go figure.

Cats do all this stuff and they're considered great.

Guys are aloof, detached, indifferent, independent, wasteful, indolent and natural and where does it get us? What's a guy gotta do?

Chapter 47

Running In the Moonlight

We had driven 2500 miles across the country to get to California and we pulled into the Malibu RV Park on Pacific Coast Highway. Amy and Brad flew in from Albuquerque and Alan drove down from Berkeley, all of us there to attend Kenton and Lulu's wedding. Five of us were going to make our bed together in our 28-foot fifth-wheel trailer.

Alan was given the dinette as his bed, and Brad and Amy were on the sofa bed. We were up front in the queen-size bed. Canoe had to find a place wherever a cat can find his rest. No problem with five people and all their accompanying luggage which provided a veritable seamless field of bodies, luggage, pillows, gift wrapping and cereal boxes. It was an idealized junkyard of bodies, odors, left- over food, fermenting garbage and hills of arms, legs, breasts and thighs. Canoe is no respector of persons or parts and he would just as soon walk on a person as avoid them.

There were numerous noises in the campground, which kept Canoe spooked and amused for most of the night. He'd run from window to window, trespassing over snoring bodies and frumpled luggage, interrupting the sleep of our houseguests who expressed their unhappiness with quiet cursing. His trampling of our bed and his flinching weirdness finally caught my attention and wrath. I listened as he bounded through the trailer, my uneasiness and annoyance growing by the minute.

Rather than consult with Eva on what to do with him, a conversation that I was sure would end up with a 4:30 a.m. argument that could be worse than the ceaseless ramblings of a neurotic cat, I decided to get up quietly, grab Canoe by the scruff of the neck, and move outside with him and place him in his carrier at the foot of the steps.

Canoe was submissive enough as I stepped outside in my nightshirt cradling the black and white cat, but as he reluctantly entered the cage and my grasp loosened, he bounded out in a flash, obviously surmising that being outside in a plastic prison with all manner of camp cats, mountain lions, wild dogs, raccoons, skunks and prehistoric monsters coming to sniff, hiss, growl or bite, was not as good as finding his own asylum in the hillside chaparral. So he did what any unreasonable cat would do. He bolted ... between the trailers and up the slope and soon he was a faint image on my screen. He was moving and he wasn't looking back.

This put me in an untenable situation. I had to go back inside and tell the MOTHER, who was wondering what I was up to, that the cat was somewhere in the campground, up a steep lope full of various thorny, scratchy and grasping things like poison oak, wild raspberry and ceanothus, and I had lost site of him.

No, she did not say, "Well then, why don't you come to bed and we'll make love." She reluctantly got her robe on and now two adults stood in nightclothes outside the trailer with the messy luggage and the guests sleeping on the sofa and the dinette; except that now they also were witnesses to the breakout because we were outside talking in muffled tones, which wakes up campers quicker than anything.

I went back inside, pulled on jeans over my nightshirt, slipped into tennis shoes, grabbed the flashlight and began the search among several hundred campers. I followed the campground road up to the next tier where Canoe had disappeared, sweeping the light through camper sewer lines, bicycles, grills and lawn chairs. I moved as quietly as a person can move over gravel in the middle of the night, trying not to look like a bandit less some big burly guy in boxer shorts and a beer belly and a tattoo with "Shirley" on his upper arm comes rumbling out of one of these trailers demanding an explanation.

Meanwhile, Eva was still standing outside the trailer, mewing sweetly, "Here, kitty kitty, C'mere Canoe. C'mon home kidder, kidder." After minutes of sweet invitations she climbed the steep Malibu hill with the thorny bushes and the grappling vines and made it to the top where he had disappeared. Apparently the sweet invitation to come home was greater than the impulse to escape, so he came to her and she bundled him in her arms and stood there in the moonlight, while I shone my flashlight and caught her from a distance. She looked like the *Lady of Fatima* with a cat. An hour had passed.

Amy in the meantime, also yielded to maternal instincts, and was outside with a plastic container full of dry cat food, shaking it like a baby rattle. I told her that the MOTHER had found him and was on her way back down to us.

By 5:30 a.m. the morning the sky was beginning to lighten,

and five people crowded in a 28-foot fifth-wheel trailer that was fermenting like over-ripe fruit were asleep for the second time. And a black and white cat called Canoe, seeing the morning light decided it was time for him to sleep too. He had had his romp in the night. He had to get ready for the next long night. Yikes!

Chapter 48

By Ourselves We Are Nothing.
With a Cat, We're Stars.

My wife can't imagine traveling only with me. I get grumpy and difficult; the cat is always sociable and kind. The cat is a softening intermediary, a third party peacemaker.

Also, a cat is a catalyst for new friendships. Numerous times during our travels I'd come back to the boat at a marina and Eva would be out walking Canoe. There would be a cluster of people gushing over his cute baby face, his silky fur and his enormous bulk. At 15 pounds and with the hide of a fluffy Holstein, he's difficult to miss, and when you stoop down to pet him and he raises his head and bleats his welcome, you know you've found a friend.

I've seen Canoe in the embrace of strange women who were cheek to cheek with him, the poor thing literally being squashed with love. He digs it, or at least he tolerates it.

We were cruising the Erie Canal and, of course, Canoe was with us. With a name like Canoe, you'd think he'd be a perfect waterman, but he's really a wuss. When we start the engine, Canoe is in the berth finding comfort and solace away from the noise.

But when the engine stops, and particularly when evening comes, Canoe comes to life. We put his halter on and take him for a walk. The more he walks the better he sleeps, and the better we sleep. But walking is a sometime thing. As soon as we walk along the waterfront with him, someone notices and says, "Look, they're actually walking their cat." This is Canoe's cue to go limp, lie on his side, look at them as if they were space ogres and make a fool of us. So we pick him up, get him away from people, put him down again and try to continue our walk. We have about a 65% frustration rate.

Apparently people find it incredible that there is a woman with a cat next to a boat. I don't understand this. Lots of people travel with cats on board, but Canoe, lying lovely on a leash, is somehow amazing. Especially for kids.

We were in Fairport, New York, on the Erie Canal and a man and his daughter were sauntering by. The 6-year-old girl couldn't stop looking at Canoe, then came over to touch him. She stroked him and he seemed to enjoy it, or tolerate it, depending on the barometric pressure or the Dow Jones. Who knows? Sometimes he looks so disinterested I wonder how the relationship keeps going; but kids don't demand much and they continue to stroke Canoe and he looks everywhere but in their direction. The parents eventually entice the kid away, but this little girl returned again and again, pulling her daddy towards Canoe, then leading his hand to stroke Canoe.

Even grownups turn into something other than rational creatures when they see Canoe on the boardwalks. They'll stop their conversations midstream and slobber some meaningless blabber.

People with animals become stars through their animals. Observers ask the name of the pet, the breed, how old? Where did you get him? Pet owners eagerly describe their breed, how they are the coolest, the fastest, the best mouse catchers, and the greatest with kids. We have our own stories about Canoe, except he ain't got no pedigree. He may be a Norwegian Forest Cat. Or maybe he's a Maine coon. For certain, he's an East Tennessee Campground Cat. Canoe speaks for himself.

Eva walks with Canoe on a halter and leash. 'Works if you go where he wants to go.

Chapter 49

Hot Beef on a Hoagie Roll

It was our last day on the Erie Canal. We'd spent the night at Lockport and settled in for the final glide into Tonowanda. About noon, our bellies began to growl and we thought about what was left in the refrigerator for lunch.

"How about those leftover beef sandwiches from Harry's in Brockport?" I suggested to Eva.

"They won't be good cold," she said.

"Okay, I'll heat 'em up," I said, and turned over the wheel of our cruiser to Eva.

Down in the galley I got out the food, placed in it in a fry pan and tried lighting the alcohol stove with the butane lighter. The front pot was dry and cold, so I tried lighting the rear one. Same thing. We had been cooking on them the entire trip and obviously they needed to be refueled.

I took the front pot out, placed in on the counter and poured alcohol from the half-full gallon into the pot. I put the pot back in its clasps beneath the stove, then added some alcohol to the back burner as well without removing it from the stove.

Apparently it was lit. A giant ball of flame leapt from the

stove and swept across the ceiling. I ran from the galley to the cockpit, dropping the half-full gallon of alcohol on the counter which glugged away feeding the flames that engulfed the galley to the ceiling, igniting a dishtowel and curtains.

Eva screamed, "Ron, do something! Throw some water on it!"

But the bucket was down in the inferno. Impulsively I shouted, "Where's the fire extinguisher?" (I should have known. I installed it.)

Eva instantly reached inside the cabin where one of the fire extinguishers lived, tied with a small bungee cord to a bracket. She singed her hair and eyebrows in the process, but the darn thing would not come loose. She struggled with it, I struggled with it and it finally came free. I figured out what was front and back, turned to the fire, hit it with expellant and the fire died, leaving a white cloud of toxic smoke.

I dashed inside to get Canoe who was lying three feet from the stove on a seat, his golden eyes glowing in the hot acrid smoke. I grabbed him and threw him to the back deck. The half-full gallon of alcohol continued to glug away, creating pools of alcohol around the stove. I grabbed it, rushed to the back deck with it and prayed that it would not explode on the way.

Canoe, upset with all the commotion, ran back inside, his usual asylum. Dumb cat. I ran back in after him, tossed him out again and followed him, sucking all the fresh air that existed in those parts. I peered back inside. The fire had re-started. I hit it with the fire extinguisher again, ordering Eva to turn off the engine. We drifted in the canal, the inside cabin remaining an inferno of putrid smoke and melted headliner. I ventured back down to assess the situation, grabbed a roll of paper towel and began swabbing pools of alcohol that lay beneath the burners and on the counter. Now I was wet with alcohol and the next flare up would have me looking like the Statue of Liberty (male version). My lungs ached as they filled with smoke. I opened the front hatch and asked Eva to start the engine and move slowly down the canal. Smoke billowed past us as the cabin cleared.

After a half-hour, I came up from the galley and salon that still had a dusting of gray/white residue over everything. It was time for thanksgiving, not for what happened but for what didn't happen. Thank God for fire extinguishers. We had three aboard but one was all it took to put out the fire.

Canoe was never crazy about boating. Now he was smoky, traumatized and medium rare. Shortly after the Erie Canal event, we stayed on the boat, with Canoe, at Grand Haven, Michigan, where we were seminar presenters, so Canoe had to stay with the stinkin' boat and it wasn't long before he had forgotten the galley from hell and the melting headliner.

Before the final estimate on the repair of the boat came in, Eva reassured me she wanted to redecorate the interior anyway. Isn't that sweet? My fear was that she would be calling me names from now till eternity…or not calling me at all.

The next time we go boating the headliner will be replaced, we'll have new curtains and we'll be having a cold lunch on the back deck, because Eva will not have ordered the hot beef on a hoagie roll.

As for Canoe? Poor guy, he'll simply have to trust the hands that support him. The rewards aren't always convincing, but we're bound together, for better or for worse.

Chapter 50

No Time for An Oreo Cookie

Cats are easy to take along when traveling by car, RV or boat. Unlike dogs who have to be taken to shore to take care of business (if they aren't trained to do it on a piece of carpet), the only thing a cat needs in addition to food, water, and a cozy place to curl up and nap, is a litter box. Cats don't bark or disturb the peace in an anchorage or marina. They can be left alone on the boat while you go ashore for hours, knowing that on your return the boat will look the same as when you left because the cat slept all the while.

When we were doing a fall color cruise of the Tennessee River, we stopped at Watts Bar Resort and tied to a dock that behaves like a snake. Step on any part of it, particularly toward the end, and the entire 100-foot thing goes into a dance. We arrived early in the day and let Canoe walk to shore on his halter and leash. Then we put him back in the boat while we went to dinner.

When we got back to the boat it was dark and we put Canoe back on his leash to give him some exercise so he'd let us sleep that night. He cautiously walked the dock, heading toward the ramp and shore as he had done earlier in the day. The Mother played out the thirty-foot line until it became taut, then jumped from the boat onto the dock to follow Canoe to shore. What she didn't anticipate was that her launch from the boat onto the dock set the whole thing into clattering gyrations.

When Eva got to the ramp which led to shore, she realized that the line was leading into the water. Canoe either got spooked and jumped or lost his balance on the wiggly dock and was in the drink. She began to haul the line in, hand over hand, dragging the cat through the dark water, screaming in full-blown histrionics, "Ron, the cat's in the water!"

As she dragged him through the water, he ended up under the dock and she couldn't reach him. I did not finish my milk and have another Oreo cookie. Nay, rather, I jumped up dutifully, ran along the wobbly dock and laid on my belly on the dock in the vicinity where she last saw him. I felt around and touched a soggy ball of fur, then grabbed a handful of cat and swung him out and up onto my back. Canoe made tracks across my back and onto the dock. I can show you the scars.

Canoe was cool about it. The Mother took him back to the boat, wrapped him in soft towels, cuddled and talked to him (incessantly) and held him on her lap until SHE was calm and relaxed and I had time for another Oreo cookie.

The cat was fine and he slept well that night. And so did we. For several days he was the best-behaved cat ever. Maybe we'll have to re-enact this episode every once in a while to remind him he can't live without us.

Chapter 51

It Tastes like Wood Chips and Fox Scat

We ran out of Canoe's usual Purina Cat Chow as we neared the end of our cruise on the Tennessee River so I went to Buehller's Market in Chattanooga near the municipal dock. The only thing they had was *Alley Cat*, Purina's cheap brand. It seemed to have similar ingredients – corn meal, turkey by products, chicken by-products, liver by-products, bone meal by-products, fish meal by-products and high fat; so I thought, what the heck, he ought to go for this.

I hate those cats in the ads where a snooty feline lies on a couch wearing a big bow, eats from a crystal bowl and the ad makers say it demands the best. My cat wasn't going to be one of those wussy, finicky, ungrateful brats who demands the best. My cat is a Rambo Cat who eats anything, anywhere. My cat eats while running from Dobermans, consumes whatever he can get his fangs on during floods and pestilence. My cat lives in the woods and eats mice and coons and rotting skunks. He taunts owls, runs in the moonlight and climbs trees like a cougar. My cat has an iron stomach and has a no-nonsense style that makes his keeper proud.

I poured a bowlful of the new food and sat back to watch my Rambo Cat gobble it up.

"I hate this stuff!" Canoe said. "It stinks. Look, you raised me on Friskies and Purina Cat Chow. Where's the bag with the happy-faced lady cuddling her cat? I got used to that. Why do you insist on making me a world survivor by putting stuff on my plate you wouldn't feed to your …cat? You say it looks like Cheerios, but it tastes like wood chips and fox scat. I refuse."

And he did. Canoe looked sorrowful at the bowl of Alley Cat food, and went, "Pffftttt." Actually, he went beyond that. He hit the bowl, batting it around like it needed to be killed. When it was turned over and the food was scattered all around the floor of the boat and it felt like glass shards on our bare feet, he'd grin and leap up on the table. He wore his usual sly, peaceful pussy cat demeanor, but we knew that he had a moment of rattling rebellion as he scattered his food to the wind with the thought of never toothing one of those hard nuggets again.

When we got home from the boat trip, we succumbed out of pity, love and weakness, and again bought the Chow with the sweet lady on the bag. We were tired of cleaning up his protest and we empathized with his demand that he eat something besides (the equivalent of) broccoli and Brussel sprouts. But we still had the bag of cheap Alley Cat and we thought of ways of blending it in with the good stuff, or….

Maybe the squirrels will eat it, we thought. "Look, Hon, the squirrels like this stuff. We can feed it to the squirrels."

Canoe sat off in a corner watching. In the game of wills and wits, it was Canoe - 10, Ron - 1. Quit smirking, Canoe.

Chapter 52

The Devil is in the Cat

You can't convince me cats don't have a sense of humor, and a sense of mischief. They've got a code of acceptable/unacceptable behavior, just like a small kid who knows when he's screwing up or misbehaving.

When Canoe comes in early from his evening rambles, let's say when it's raining, he still has a half a tank of adventure left in him and there are only finite ways of getting it vented and spent. When he comes in, he'll bleat his usual; "I'm home. You guys here?"

We'll respond with greetings, then it's back to the paper or the computer or the television for us, and Canoe will sit there like a taxidermist's model surmising, "Well so much for fun on the senior frontier. Now what do I do? These people are soooo dull."

He reckons sooner than later that he has to play by himself because the two big dopes on the sofa aren't going to get up.

I take that back. Eva who is more responsive to him than I am will get up and look at him and they'll talk and she'll sense that he's restless. She'll get the fishing pole with the mouse-on-an-elastic string-thing out and Canoe will get excited with the moving, jerking mouse wiggling across the carpeting, around the chair and over the top of the sofa. He's a sucker for this and he'll go for this mouse until he gets his teeth and claws in it. But he'll release it because he realizes this is a game. This can go on until he tires of it, then nothing will get him going again…until we walk away from him and go back to our viewing or reading, then like a small kid who's gotten his second-wind back, he'll go looking for excitement again.

He walks the kitchen counters, which I hate, because he's been who knows where and he's leaving pads of exotic bacteria and viruses all over the counters. I'll holler, "Canoe, get down." He'll act like he never heard those words before.

I'll bellow, "Canoe, get down."

Nothing.

I'll SCREAM, "Canoe, get down!"

"You were calling, sire?"

"Yes, you meathead. Get down."

"Now?"

"Yes, now."

"On the dining room side of the counter, or the kitchen side?"

By this time I can't stand his impertinence any longer and I'm launching myself out of my complacency.

"Oh, okay, I'll get down," he says.

I want to wring his neck, but he's scampered down the stairs to the lower level.

In about the time it takes me to regain normal breathing and heart rate, Canoe is back upstairs…on the counter, pushing things off with his nose – telephone books (PLOP), the mail, pens, pencils. Then he'll drop to the floor with a thump of fifteen pounds of cat smacking the floor and use these objects as hockey pucks or sticks to kick.

He'll jump onto the piano and nudge off the binoculars and the bird book. Some of this stuff is valuable. We don't want it dropped or rearranged.

The ritual has become predictable with us who love him (well, love is a bit strong), and we chase him with the urge to SMACK HIM. As he runs away we can hear him giggle.

Don't tell me that cats are without a sense of humor.

Chapter 53

Canoe Loves Birds

Canoe loves birds. And so do we. Therein lies the problem. We wonder if we will ever change his nature from hunter to peaceful observer. This may be as easy as selling a Tennessee hunter membership in the Sierra Club.

"Of course, you can't take the hunter out of a cat," you say. "You're trying to make a Holstein out of a feline."

Well, it can be done. At least I'm going ahead with this notion. But I have to admit, I'm not making big strides in that direction. Anything that moves not only evokes curiosity for Canoe, but the desire, nay, the mandate, to catch it.

"Look, Ron," Canoe says, "God wants me to hunt and kill. This is the way He made me."

The technique I use to change his habit about free and wild creatures is one you're sure to want to learn, so listen up. It's saying, "No, No, No," every time you see your cat at the bird feeder. Pretty easy, eh? Then you proceed to pick up your cat and take it inside and repeat the "No, No, No," commands. That's it.

After years of research I'm here to tell you…this does not

make a bit of difference. But I'm happy to report that I think it gives your cat a complex. Now when I see Canoe at the feeder on the back deck, I head out and as soon as Canoe hears the door open, he's down the stairs and out of sight. He knows he's doing wrong.

He can show up in the house fifteen minutes later and wrap around my legs, which suggests he holds no grudges, which is cool because I want a nice relationship with my cat. But the efficacy of this technique is about as good as telling a teenage kid to drive carefully. "Okay, Dad, I'll be careful." Sure.

One morning I saw Canoe outside at the feeder that was crowded with goldfinches. They were hungry after a night in the woods and even the presence of a cat who was as still as a figurine didn't dissuade them. One quick strike and he'd have one of those babies in his mouth, then he'd run off somewhere, maybe back into the house through the garage door and "play" with it. We'd see the results of this freeplay, which always included a lot of feathers indicating the struggle, and a wet and lifeless body.

So I headed out the bedroom door onto the deck, heading off Canoe's escape down the flight of stairs. He bolted like a thief when he saw me, but I had his exit blocked. He tried a run around. I dodged and bolted like a quarter horse cornering a calf. He tried another run around. I adjusted and Canoe gave up.

You know the feeling when the old man catches you reading a girly magazine or sneaking a cookie and you just have to stand there and take it? In humans, guilt floods over us and there is an overwhelming feeling of shame and sorrow. We wait for the executioner to give us our sentence, our heads drooped, our eyes downcast.

Same with cats. Canoe stopped dead in his tracks, faced

the woods and let me approach. I grabbed him by the nape of the neck to let him know who's boss, then picked him up and took him inside repeating the "No, NO, NO" message and somewhere in there getting in the word, "birds."

I've done this repeatedly and after years of diligent work, I'm not too happy to report that there is no sign of reform, no change of heart. But I think he's feeling guilty. That's some kind of win, isn't it?

Chapter 54

Canoe Tries Flying

We've got some new critters in the woods. Canoe was out patrolling one night and spotted them at the bird feeder. We went looking for him and there he was, eyeball to eyeball with two nocturnal flying squirrels (Glaucomas volans) at our feeder suspended on a limb of the beech tree. We were thrilled. So was Canoe. Problem was he was interested in hunting; we were interested in simply having them in the neighborhood.

He was perched on the railing and within a breath of the little creatures, but there was a gap between them that was two-feet wide and 20 feet straight down. He apparently realized that if he were to lurch for one, he'd be clinging to the big beech tree and his prey simultaneously. Then, of course, the problem would be how to get back to the launch site on the deck rail.

In time, with regular feeding and despite Canoe's threatening vigil, the squirrels kept coming back. We could just about set our watches to the squirrel's arrival. There was an entire clan. Five of the little guys, beady-eyed and quick as lightning, sailing onto the tree or soaring away to distant trees.

They climb to high limbs in neighboring trees, then glide down to the beech tree with the feeder. They always glide from high to low, their white underbellies flashing as they swoop upward onto vertical tree trunks. There's no flapping, simply gliding, their outstretched legs connected with a flap of skin between their "wrists and ankles."

There's a pecking order among the squirrels with some of the lesser ones being scolded by the bigger ones, but eventually little squirrel bellies fill and the tension decreases until they've all had satisfaction.

They eat like regular tree squirrels, posing endearingly on their haunches with little paws grasping seeds, in this case sunflower seeds, as they de-hull them.

When our grown kids were in town they watched the squirrels as evening deepened, then moved onto the deck to get a closer look. I was down below on the ground observing five humans within touching distance of the squirrels. The squirrels were going about their business as though these people were mannequins. I had observed the squirrels deferentially, staying inside and observing them with a flashlight. Now I go outside when they are there, fill the feeder in their presence, stand back a few feet and watch them proceed with dinner.

Squirrels are easily domesticated and become accustomed to people. We could probably make pets of them. But then, we already have one. Better they have the forest as their home than a cage in our house. An animal free to be whatever it is, is a more marvelous thing to behold than one kept prisoner.

Flying squirrels have strong maternal instincts. There are accounts of flying squirrel mothers who followed researchers who had removed a nest and babies from the crotch of a tree and placed the babies in a box. Without hesitation, the mother jumped into the box and ran off with her babies, one at a time, until all were safely secured in a new nest. They have even been known to run up the leg of a researcher who is holding their baby and snatch it, run down the leg and away.

Meanwhile, Canoe sits atop the rail watching and twitching excitedly. At times he's on the verge of a launch, but the yellow light turns to red and he hesitates. Aggressive moods and actions from him bring on a scurry of activity from the squirrels, some of them bailing out and gliding to neighboring trees. But it isn't long before they're back. Their actions are so quick it takes a determined and attentive person (or cat) to catch the flight. It all happens in fractions of seconds. Their usual flight is 50-60 feet but the record is 150 feet.

Canoe changes his position frequently on the deck rail, trying to get enough substance beneath his hind limbs for a launch. He'll quiver with excitement, his tail swishing, his legs taut. Eventually, he turns around as if to say, "I don't want to look at you squirrels. You're driving me nuts. I'm going inside."

We haven't located the squirrel nests, but they're likely to be in hollow trees, several of which exist in the woods. We've read reports where as many as 26 squirrels were found in one hollow tree.

With our larder always full, the flying squirrels are likely to increase in numbers over the years and Canoe is likely to have many evenings sitting on the rail of the deck observing his little friends. With a life span of 7-13 years they could become like locusts. But owls, foxes and cats are likely to catch some of these, cutting their life expectancy in the wild to 5-6 years. We just hope it's not Canoe that shortens their lives. We've told him so.

Chapter 55

Shooting a Cat

If Canoe was going to be on the cover of this book, he ought to be photographed in a canoe. After all…

So we went into the dungeon, the lowest level of the house where the canoe, lawn furniture and garden stuff lives, and pulled the canoe into the light, then down the slope through the woods to the docks on the cove of the Little Tennessee River.

The plan was to have Eva on the dock photographing with two cameras. Canoe was to get into the canoe with me and I was to position the canoe so Canoe would be in a favorable light perched on the bow looking longingly, we supposed, toward shore.

After we brought the canoe down to the water Eva went back up to get the photographic gear and a sleepy Canoe who was curled like a croissant and groggy from dreams. By the time she arrived at the cove, I was already in the canoe and waiting for him.

Eva transferred him to me and I gave him a reassuring hug, then put him on the floor of the canoe while simultaneously shoving away to prevent him from returning to the dock.

Now he was really awake as we drifted away and I began to slowly paddle farther away until I could circle back and orient him and the canoe for favorable composition while Eva got the cameras ready.

As a precaution I took along a big towel just in case Canoe ended up in the water. If he fell in, I reasoned, I would throw the towel toward him, he would cling to it, I would bring the towel toward the boat and slurp him back in. I also took along a life jacket so that I could throw it and he would have something to cling to. Or maybe I would have something to don in case I went in after him. I was fearful that a panicky cat might bail out and then choose the far shore of the cove for refuge. If this became the situation he would be in the water for some time and with the water temperature around 50 degrees on this late December day he could become hypothermic. So could I.

The shoot was nearly professional, Eva alternated between cameras to get good candids of Canoe in the bow of the canoe, something like the portrait of George Washington crossing the Delaware.

But Canoe was not content to stand or sit on the seat; he got up on the tip of the canoe, the aluminum shield that covered the bow. This did not provide any toeholds and there was nothing for his soft pads or his clawed toes to grasp. My movements became fluid and cautionary. I talked to him reassuredly positioning the canoe near the docks and getting ever closer so Eva could get a full frame shot. I came within a few inches of the dock and that was enough for Canoe. He launched and was in her lap before she could say, "Ron, he's going to jump!"

But she had him and I sidled next to the dock to retrieve him and put him back in the canoe for more paddling around the dock while Eva photographed.

Canoe studied the water studiously, watching the swirls created by the paddles, looking to shore, watching Eva on the dock. Everything was tantalizingly close, yet far away.

He leaned far over the bow towards the water and I suspected he might jump. "NO, NO, NO, Canoe!" I implored. "Don't you dare jump. I don't want to go in after you."

But it was too late. He launched. Well, more like he just slipped in head first leaving hardly a splash. He was fully submersed, out of sight, then came up, shaking the water from his head and paddling toward shore like a retriever.

"I am not going to put up with that dumb canoe anymore," he was muttering, "I'll take my chances getting to shore on my own."

He didn't head for the finger pier where Eva was (he'd already been there), but rather made a beeline for the next one. I didn't panic, although Eva was having histrionics running along the bridge of the dock to the shoreline finger where Canoe was headed. She called, he paddled, I followed slowly in the canoe. Did he go towards her? Of course not. She was part of the conspiracy. We were not his refuge and his strength in time of trouble. In time of hunger? Maybe, but his trust was in himself.

He reached the dock and in an instant climbed onto the floats that suspend the dock. I think that as soon as he got himself out of the water and onto the float and saw that he was still fifteen feet from shore and he'd have to relaunch, he had a little internal dialogue…"NUTS, I didn't go far enough. What am I going to do now? Can I move to adjacent floats and then make it to shore? Not without getting back in the water. Do I want to get back into the canoe with the big guy? I don't think so. I need time to figure this out…hmmm."

I pulled alongside and was within touching distance. We talked for a while…okay, I talked he listened, but he wasn't moving and he was thinking. "No, sir, I am not going back in your stupid canoe. You think this is a lot of fun. Well, let me tell you, buster, water is anathema to me, water is trouble, water is wet, water is something I avoid at all costs even if it means I have to get in it to escape it. I know that doesn't make sense to you, but cats have their reasons and their phobias. You have your traditions; cats have theirs. You get wet every morning and I don't know of a cat that thinks this is cool. You may own me, but you don't own my life or my actions or my wants or my needs or what scares the heck out of me and…."

"Oh, shut up already! You had your way and now you're sitting underneath this finger pier on this float. This is a nice hideaway, isn't it? You could freeze to death here. I'm trying to help you."

"Yeah, thanks a lot. It's so nice to see you again. Now go away. I want to sulk."

Canoe eyed his options, looking to shore, eyeing the next set of floats that required a reentry into the water. His options were limited.

I kept my position in the canoe tied to the finger dock, then took the towel and spread it across the black vinyl surface of the float. This tactile surface allowed Canoe to get his feet and claws into something substantial and he came to it, flicked his paws and situated himself onto it as if it were a rug by the fireplace.

I gently stroked him, then grasped a front leg and pulled him towards the edge of the float and back into the canoe. The alpha male insisted and he submitted.

I kept the bow of the canoe snubbed to the dock and let him move forward in the canoe where he saw his escape – a jump up onto the dock where Eva was waiting. I tossed her the towel and she let loose with psychobabble and gently massages with the towel. She went up the hill with a 15-pound – no, make that an 18-pound cat now that he was soaked – for drying and a little lovin'. I pulled the canoe out of the water and called it a day. The shoot was over.

Canoe (the cat) was hardly wet. His downy undercoat kept him buoyant and warm and there wasn't any evidence that this was a horrendous emotional event. Of course, how do we know? Swimming came as naturally to him as peeing in a litter box.

Now we wonder when we're traveling with him in the boat and he's walking the deck or sitting on the bow if he might just say, "I need a break from this boat and these people." Then plunk, he'll be in the water making for shore and Eva will be screaming, "Ron, Canoe's in the water. Go get him!"

Canoe looks off the back of the boat.
Is he thinking of going in?

Chapter 56

Timeless and True

In a world of e-commerce, wireless phones and impersonal communications, family pets continue to fill our most basic needs. What makes cats so attractive to us is because they are simple and without disguises. Cats aren't into salesmanship, politics and popularity. Possession of clothes and accumulated wealth means nothing to them. They operate on primitive instincts and they amuse us with behavior as elemental as looking, touching and licking.

A cat's life feeds from the primordial messages in the limbic system. They lick their paws, then lick their anuses. They lie discreetly and squint through sultry eyes, then roll over and expose themselves unashamedly. We may feed them from a crystal chalice, but they would just as soon drink from the toilet.

They give no heed to world affairs or company mergers or the rise and fall of the DOW or the NASDAQ. They live for the moment, for a pat, a cuddling, a morsel of food, a place in the sun, a romp in the yard.

Cats don't know or care what kind of day we've had or where we've been. They don't know if we have dirty thoughts or clean thoughts or no thoughts at all. They're just happy to see us. The moment at hand is what counts. The person comes home, prepares the evening meal, reads the paper and shuffles through a variety of routines and the cat sprawls across the floor and watches and waits.

We put our face to theirs and we talk baby talk and make innocent love. The Annuity and Life Specialist, the Divisional Director of Sales, the Administrative Assistant for Development is seduced to animal nakedness. We become infantile, lovable and guileless.

There are no Republican cats or Democratic cats or Libertarian cats. They're neutral or nothing on politics because the pulse of life does not beat there.

Telephones and email take the place of close personal relationships in our lives. The mall has replaced the woods as the place to play. There are no swings in the trees. We flit and flirt with everything; we're day traders in our affections. But the cat and the family dog remain old-fashioned and true. They represent the swing in the big tree, a ramble in a streambed looking for salamanders, a romp in a mound of fallen leaves in October. They represent the goodness of life that hasn't changed.

Cats exemplify the love of God – always there, timeless, forever, till death do us part. Cats teach us forgiveness, for despite our forgetfulness in feeding them, our indifference to their needs, our inattention to their existence, they come to us without remorse or bitterness. They show us gratitude when gratitude wasn't earned. They exhibit play when all hell breaks loose, or we're dying, or life seems bleak and hopeless. They teach us the magic of touch and the romance of simply being in space, patient and still, waiting for companionship.

Thank you, Lord, for our cats and dogs who show us sincerity in a world of gamesmanship; who teach us the pleasure of simple things when we seek the exotic and expensive; who exhibit faithfulness when all around us people are playing one against the other. We're happy for their unconditional affection. Our pets are our teachers, our inspiration and our best friends. Thank you for the beauty of your creation and the presence of animals in our lives.

Canoe loves to play in the pile of glittery gold
Christmas tree garlands.

About
Canoe's
Authors

Ron Stob was a travel writer and photographer for the San Luis Obispo County (California) *Telegram-Tribune* from 1984 through 1998, taking readers on hikes, river-rafting excursions and motor trips along the back roads in search of the obscure and unusual. He has written books on travel from Santa Barbara to Big Sur — *Back Roads of the Central Coast, More Back Roads of the Central Coast* and *Exploring San Luis Obispo and nearby coastal areas.*

He and his wife, Eva, write and photograph for a variety of publications, including *Heartland Boating, Highways, Power and Motoryacht, Latitudes & Attitudes, Trailer Boats Magazine, Go Boating, Wildlife Conservation* and *Bluegrass Unlimited.* Their photographs often appear on magazine covers.

The Stob's have traveled throughout all 50 of the United States and abroad. Together, they learned about boats and cruised for nearly a year aboard their forty-foot trawler, *Dream O'Genie.* Their book, *"Honey, Let's Get a Boat...": A Cruising Adventure of America's Great Loop*, is the story of their 6300-mile cruise encompassing 145 locks around Eastern North America, known as the Great Loop or Great Circle Cruise.

In 1999, they formed America's Great Loop Cruisers' Association, a network of boaters who cruise or dream of cruising the coastal and inland waterways of Eastern North America. (Visit website at www.greatloop.com.)

Ron and Eva reside with their cat, Canoe, along the shores of the Little Tennessee River on Tellico Lake in the hills of East Tennessee. They travel and discover America's scenic areas in their 5th-wheel travel trailer, and explore the inland waterways in their trailerable cruiser, *Li'l Looper*, taking Canoe with them on most trips. He has visited more states than most people and has endured more miles beneath his paws then he cares to think about.

Other books by Ron Stob

Back Road of the Central Coast
More Back Roads of the Central Coast
Exploring San Luis Obispo County and nearby coastal areas
"Honey, Let's Get a Boat...": A Cruising Adventure of
America's Great Loop

(To order more copies of this book,
use Order Form on reverse side.)

Order Form

For postal orders, send completed form with check, money order or credit card information to:

    Raven Cove Publishing
    P. O. Box 168
    Greenback, TN 37742-0168, USA

Telephone orders: 865/856-7888
Fax orders: 865/856-7889
For inquiries by E-mail: REStob@aol.com
Website: http://hometown.aol.com/restob/raven/htm

— — — — — — — — — — — — — — — — — — — —

Please send ___ copies of *A Cat Called Canoe* @ $12.95ea.(U.S.$;
    No foreign checks, please.) $12.95 x (#) ___= $ _____
S&H: U.S.: $3.00 - book rate (media mail); $5.00 -priority mail.
    Canada: $7.00; Int'l: $9.00. Add $2.00 for ea. additional
    book shipped to same address.   Shipping = $ _____
                                    Subtotal = $ _____
Sales tax: Add 9.00% for books shipped to Tennessee addresses.
                        Tax, if applicable = $ _____

Ship to: Payment Total = $ _____
Name: _____
Address: _____
City: _____ State: ___ Zip: _____
Telephone: _____
E-mail: _____
  Payment by: (Circle one) Check Money Order Credit card
Charge my credit card: Visa MasterCard AmExp Discover
Card #: _____
Expiration Date: _____
Cardholder Name: _____
Signature:
_____